Dog Only Knows

Dog Only Knows
(The Word of Dog)

by

as Translated from the Original Dog by Terry Kaye
Illustrations by Kat McDonough

Mill City Press, Minneapolis

Mill City Press, Inc.
322 First Avenue N, 5th floor
Minneapolis, MN 55401
612.455.2293
www.millcitypublishing.com

For more love, laughter, and lessons straight from the dog's mouth, visit Belle at dogonlyknows.com

ISBN-13: 978-1-63505-153-7
LCCN: 2016904286

Printed in the United States of America

To my parents, Saralee and Marvin Kaye, whose love of the written word and the awful pun were passed on to me at a very early age, and whose inspiration and support are the pillars on which this book was built.

Terry Kaye, translator

To all Peoples, whom I love with my whole spirit, and especially to my Person, who not only listens to me, but also hears me.

BELLE, author

Contents

A NOTE FROM THE TRANSLATOR

When my dog told me she wanted to write a book, I naturally thought she was joking. After all, I am pretty sure she's never even read a book. Eaten them, yes. Read? Not so much.

But once I realized she was serious, I started thinking, it's not such a bad idea. After all, I speak Dog, and I do have those opposable thumbs that enable me to type on a keypad. So I asked her to dictate a couple of chapters to me, to see what was on her mind. And I've got to say, I was impressed. I think dogs and humans alike could benefit from some of her insights.

I've always said that Belle is too smart for my own good. When she was a baby, the size of my shoe, she figured out how to get out of her playpen because she wanted to be where the people were. When she couldn't reach her favorite toy, instead of crying for me to get it for her, she'd stop and think about it, until she figured out how to go around a different way and get it herself. You could almost see the wheels turning in her head. And somehow she always knows to shred the last thirty pages of a mystery novel.

For the most part, I've tried to translate literally without editing, but you will find occasional footnotes from me. And I do want to remind you that the points of view expressed in this work are the opinions of the author, and not necessarily those of the translator.

That being said, I've got to tell you, she's pretty spot on about a lot of things. Our relationship is constantly evolving, and as much as she's learned from me, I've learned double from her. While Belle's primary objective here is to educate and entertain her canine audience, I believe that humans will benefit greatly from her wisdom. If you have a dog, are considering getting a dog, or just plain like dogs, this book is for you.

Regards,

Terry

A NOTE FROM THE AUTHOR

So here's the thing: I am a dog. Being a dog, I have learned certain things about the world in which we all live. I am thrilled to have the opportunity to share these lessons with you, my fellow canines in the hope that I might help you find your way through this wide, wonderful world.

Now, I'm not talking about the basic stuff, like how to sit or stay or lie down. I feel pretty confident in saying that most of you who are reading this already know how to do that. Whether you choose to do so or not, well, that's your prerogative. Remember, though: you have to choose your battles. Choose wisely!

But I am getting ahead of myself. I guess what I am really trying to say is that, with a little effort and a lot of finesse, you can reach a true, deep understanding with your person that will enrich both of your lives.

In a nutshell, training is a two-way street. Yes, you will master sit and stay, you may learn to roll over, shake paws, even tap dance if your person is really ambitious. But your owner will learn from you, too, if you teach them well.

There are things that are patently clear to us as dogs that humans just don't get unless it's spelled out for them. I am not saying they're stupid. You just have to remember, they are people. They are wired differently. So in order for them to learn, you have to put things in terms they can understand.

I know, that may sound speciesist of me. I don't mean it that way. I love my person! In fact, I love all people—well, except that guy who delivers newspapers in our building at three in the morning. Him I don't trust as far as I could fetch him. But that's not the point. People are wonderful, loving creatures. They just need to be trained.

A properly trained human is kind of like a tall, furless dog. Sometimes I think my person believes she is a dog. In a lot of ways, she kind of is. I'm still working on a couple of problem areas, but I think she's really starting to get it. And your person can too!

You will notice that at times during this narrative, I address my canine audience directly; at other moments, I speak to their human counterparts. Occasionally, I may talk to both of you at once. I trust you are all smart enough to figure it out. So, on that note, read on, and enjoy!

Love and face licks,

YOU CAN LEAD A
DOG TO WATER . . .

Let's start with that old adage. You know, the one with horses and water, and how you can't make them drink? I find that this is extremely applicable to the canine situation.

Now, of course, there is the literal. If I am thirsty, I will drink. If not, I won't. You're smart enough to figure that out. But I would like to point out a few parallels:

1. You can lead a dog to grass, but you cannot make it pee.

I cannot tell you how many times I have been dragged outside to a patch of grass and my person stands there with this expectant look on her face. She'll even go so far as to tell me to "do my stuff," take my "pee break," or some such nonsense.

To which I ask: Have I ever brought you into the bathroom and told you to pee? I don't think so![1]

---

1 Translator's note: Belle informs me that her practice of following me into the bathroom does not count. According to her, the point is that I went in there of my own free will, and the fact that she sits there staring at me is irrelevant.

Furthermore, do you think I haven't noticed that you always bring me outside to pee right before you go out and leave me alone? Perhaps, if you listened to me, you might realize that my refusal to pee is really a plea—it's a pee plea! I am gambling on the idea that if I don't pee, you won't leave.

Of course, I have been wrong on this and found myself back in the apartment unpeed and alone for several hours. My own fault, yes, but really, you can't blame a dog for trying!

This is the first rule of Dog: I don't ever want you to leave me! Much of what I do comes back to this simple fact. I only have certain methods open to me to communicate this to you. Pee retention is one of these methods, albeit not the best nor the most successful one.

To my fellow dogs, I must stress that last fact and encourage you to carefully evaluate the situation before you try this strategy. Be honest with yourself, and weigh the desire for company against the current fullness of your bladder. If you really need to go, go. There will be other, better ways to get your point across later! Trust me on this.

2. You can lead a dog to the park, but you cannot make it play.

Don't get me wrong, I love the park, and I love to play as much as the next pooch. I'm just saying that there's no need to get upset if I am not running like a demon every second we are at the park. Sometimes, a good roll in the grass or a nice sprawl in the shade is all I need.

And as you are well aware, even in the middle of a great game of fetch, sometimes it's just time to stop and lick a face.

I get this argument all the time: "You could lie down at home; we come here so you can run! So go run! Run like a crazy dog!"

Really?

If it's 90 degrees out there, I would have to be a crazy dog to run like a crazy dog.

So I ask you this: Do we go to the park for me or for you? Since it's called a dog park, I'm guessing it's for me. As such, I will use it as I see fit. When I am ready to run I will bring you a ball! Which leads me to my next point:

3. You can lead a dog to a ball, but you cannot make it fetch.

Why, oh why, oh *why* does it bother people when they throw the ball and I don't go get it? I just got it seventeen times, you really need number eighteen? Dude, I am on a break! Get it yourself!

IS IT A GOOD THING
OR A BAD THING?

There are so many things in this world that it can be confusing sometimes. So many smells out there. So many objects, plants, animals, people . . . A maze of sensory input, if you will, vast and difficult to navigate. Without a method of prioritizing, you can easily get lost in the labyrinth. But never fear—I am going to show you the way.

It all starts with this: you have to be able to differentiate between what is Not Good and what is Good. It's that simple. Is it Good? Then go for it! Is it Not So Good? Leave it and find something better.

I have come up with a simple checklist that will immediately determine whether an object is worth the effort. I call it my "Is It Good?" list, and I am telling you, it's foolproof. If the answer to any of the following questions is yes, then it is a Good Thing.

Question 1: Can I fetch it?

The beauty of this is that soooo many things fall into this category! Tennis balls, sure, but also rope toys, plush toys, hand puppets, dish towels, slippers, and so much more!

A close corollary to this is the query, "Can I chase it?" Really, they are almost the same. The difference is that where fetching usually involves waiting for someone to throw something, chasing can be quite spontaneous and requires no waiting whatsoever.

The ultimate chase-able thing, of course, is the squirrel. This is by far the best. If I could just figure out that tree-climbing thing, I'd have caught me so many squirrels by now I wouldn't know what to do with them.

Actually, other than chasing, what *do* you do with a squirrel? Note to self: think on this.

Anyway, the point is, you can chase animals, windblown leaves, random bits of garbage, your own tail . . . The possibilities are endless. Some dogs chase a little point of light that their person flashes on the wall. Personally, I don't go in for that. You can't sink your teeth into a spot of light. It doesn't have that squirrel smell. You can't pull all the stuffing out of it after you fetch it. But hey, to each his own. It is chase-able, so it is ultimately a Good Thing.

Question 2: Can I chew it?

Once again, I have to say, this category is huge! Your person may disagree with me on this (we'll get to that later), but I say to you: there are so many chewable objects that, if you play your cards right (ooh! cards!), you may discover new chewing pleasures every day!

First and foremost, there is food. Kibble, crunchy treats, chewy treats: all are good and all involve chewing. Well, for me they do. I know a certain Australian Shepherd who doesn't seem to bother. She's like a vacuum cleaner; she sucks up that dish of food in three and a half seconds. I highly don't recommend this. Most of the taste is in the chewing. You should savor every bite. Try it, you'll like it!

Now, the world of chewing extends way beyond your dog dish. Let's talk about bones. Bones are one of the truly great pleasures of doghood. There are as many kinds of bones as you can imagine—knucklebones, rib bones, shank bones . . . There are bones that are twisted into braids and funny shapes, and there are bones that are filled with marrow.

Then there are bones that are not really bones at all, like antlers, pig ears, and bully sticks![1] All of which are awesome, because they provide hours of chewing pleasure.

For any peoples reading this who may be a little squeamish about the idea of all these bones and things, you might want to unsqueam yourself. We are carnivores (okay, we're omnivores, but we loves us some meat!), and we need to chew. It's in our nature. It's good for our teeth. And it's good for your furniture, because we'd much rather chew on that pig's ear than your couch. But in a pinch . . . Well, you get the idea.

On a personal note, I find that the best time to chew bones is when there's more than one person in the house. Not sure why that

---

1 Author's note: If you are not sure what a bully stick is, ask your person to tell you. This is a family book and I will not go into specifics here. Once you know, all I can say is, get over it! They're yummy!

is . . . It just seems like the thing to do. It's like, at the happiest, most secure moments in my life, that's when the chewing instinct calls to me. I wonder if others have experienced this? Feel free to drop me a note and share your chew-worthy moments. You never know, I could write a sequel.

Now, on to the less conventional chewing opportunities. Many dogs seem to enjoy the taste and texture of a people shoe. I admit, I experimented as a puppy, but I find that it's not worth the trouble of the subsequent scolding. Plush dog toys offer the same enjoyment without the whole haven't-I-told-you-a-thousand-times-not-to-do-that-what-am-I-going-to-do-with-you rigmarole. And (bonus!) with the plush toy, there is the extra fun of pulling out all that stuffing! Chewing is even more fun when you have a goal, and I find that the goal of defuzzing a stuffed bunny rabbit is highly rewarding and entertaining. Later you can sit in the middle of your pile of fuzz and bask in the glow of knowing that you created that work of art.

Okay, every dog has a weakness where chewing is concerned, maybe a sneaker, maybe the strap of a purse, maybe a particularly tasty piece of couch. Something that you just can't resist, even though you know your person will never understand or accept your need for chompage. My weakness is paper. Any kind of paper, although I do have a particular taste for the last thirty pages of mystery novels[2] and for important documents. I tried a $20 bill once; it wasn't bad. I have managed to curb my need for paper enough that when my person

---

2 Translator's note: Aha! I knew it wasn't an accident!

is home, I can forego it. But when I am by myself . . .in the apartment . . . lonely and bored . . .and she left out that tempting stack of crisp, chewable, shreddable paper . . .well, come on! I'm only a dog; I don't have supernatural willpower! I know I'll pay later, but darn, it's just so good! Cereal boxes . . . mail . . . magazines . . . *paper towels!*

Sorry, got a little carried away there. But this brings me to an important point: you can negotiate with your person. My person, for example, has gotten into the habit of only leaving out things that have to be shredded anyway. So, she might leave these things she calls "credit card applications" on the table and tell me, "Here's something to do while I'm out." This is a great deal for us both: I am not only satisfying my own need to shred, but I am also actually performing a needed service for her. I feel useful! And I don't get yelled at when she gets home. How cool is that?!

I also use paper shredding as a training opportunity. After all, I have been trained to know that if I sit, roll over, or shake paws, I will get praise, a treat, or a toy. So it follows, why not train my person: if you never leave me, I won't eat your stuff.[3]

I must admit, however, that my person seems to be a bit slow on this subject. No matter how many times I explain it to her, she still goes out sometimes *without me!* Sigh. I'll keep trying, although I'm starting to think maybe she's just not quite smart enough to get the concept.

Question 3: Can I lick its face?

---

[3] Author's note: For more detail on this, see chapter 11, titled, "If You Never Leave Me, I Won't Eat Your Stuff."

This is, for me, the third and final question in determining if something is a Good Thing. If I can lick its face, generally it is Good.

Some dogs lick other dogs' faces. I guess if you live together, it's like giving your sister or brother a good-night kiss. But licking strange dogs? I am not really a fan of this. If you ask me, it's a little bit bold to lick a dog's face if you don't know him. But hey, if it floats your boat, and the other dog doesn't object, lick away.

For me, the best faces for licking are people faces. And it's totally okay to lick a people face even if you've just met. Not sure why, but it just is. I guess it's an interspecies thing.

People faces are usually not furry, they have a nice salty taste, and they often do this cute laughing thing when you lick them. They are moving targets, which presents a nice challenge. And it's a great way to show respect and affection.

Some people claim that they do not want to be licked. *This is simply not true.* I am not sure why they stick to this story, although I suspect some form of brainwashing at an early age. The thing is, if they tried it, they would like it, but I don't suggest forcing them. Best course of action: continue to offer your licking services, perhaps by licking the air in their general direction or by sneaking in a quick lick when they are in licking range—like when they bend down to tie their shoe.

Fact is, there is no better way to say "I love you" to a people than to lick its face. It conveys all the emotion that you would say out loud if you could just form the words. I have been known to lick a face for five or ten minutes straight. And I could go longer. Really, I could.

Licking can also be a good attention-getting tactic. When my person is on the phone, sometimes I will stick my nose in there and lick away while she is talking, because really she should be paying attention to me, not to that phone thing. It works pretty well, usually.

I have heard my person say that my face-licking is "natural exfoliation," but I'm not sure what that means. It seems like it is a Good Thing for her, though. If anyone knows what exfoliation is, please let me know in three-syllable words or less.

So there you have it: my foolproof system of determining what is a Good Thing.

Can I fetch it? Can I chew it? Can I lick its face?

Remember these words, repeat them to yourself like a mantra, and in time it will become second nature to you. Next time you venture out into the wide, wide world, you will know, without a doubt, what the Good Things are.

ALL TOYS ARE EQUAL, BUT SOME TOYS ARE MORE EQUAL THAN OTHERS

I love my toys. Balls, plush toys, squeaky toys, rattly toys, toys that roll, toys that bounce, toys that my owner wears on her hand while we wrestle. Toys are, in a dog's world, the pot of gold at the end of the rainbow.

And, as any dog will know, toys are 100 percent the property of the dog. They are mine! I can chew them, rip them up, roll on them, slobber on them, and play with them to my heart's content. There are few things that a dog can truly call her own. My toys are, quite simply, *my* toys.

I like to have all of my toys out and about at all times. It doesn't matter if I am playing with a toy at the present moment, I will be later, and anyway, it's mine. I like it to be out on the floor. My person tends to put them away at the end of the day, which is okay I guess, but it just means that in the morning, I have to take each one out again, until they are all gloriously spread out all over the living room floor. As they should be.

My person also takes my stuff off the floor when she brings out that awful machine that makes all the noise while she walks around the apartment. I do not like it when she does this. It is a bit of a violation, really, having my stuff moved when I am right there. Sometimes I try to express my dissatisfaction by grabbing whatever she puts away and tossing it back onto the floor. But ultimately, I end up suffering the double indignity of watching my toys being unceremoniously dumped onto the shelf and suffering through the horrible noise of that utterly pointless beast of a machine. Sometimes it is hard to be me.

But back to the subject of toys. I'm sure you all have your favorites, as do I. And I wonder if you have noticed, as I have, that your favorite toy may change depending on your mood. For instance, I very much enjoy when my owner throws my ball so I can fetch it and catch it in midair. But there are times when really all I want to do is wrestle with my stuffed cow (the one she wears on her hand) or try to make my stuffed mouse squeak. What I am getting at is that, while I love all my toys equally, there are moments when only one specific toy will do, and I will not play with anything else. That's just the way it is.

At the park, we play with toys that are not our own. They live at the park and are played with by many different dogs. This presents a different set of rules and a different hierarchy of what are the best, most desirable toys.

First of all, where tennis balls are concerned, the rule of

thumb[1] is: the slimier, the better. This is true for 99 percent of all dogs. I would have said 100 percent until yesterday, when I met a dog who actually brought his tennis ball back after each fetch and dropped it in a tub of water to wash it before the next throw. I was, I admit, fascinated by this behavior. It seems to me that half of the fun is in the gloppiness[2] of the ball. I may have to try this washing thing, just once, to check it out. It's so crazy it just might work—although I highly doubt it.

For most of us, the best ball is the one that has been rolled through the grass, dirt, and mud; the one that has been chewed on by a multitude of dogs; the one that has real character to it. It strikes me as funny that my person never seems to want to touch this ball. After all, I put it in my mouth, and I'm just fine with it.

The law of supply and demand also comes into play at the dog park. Quite simply, if there is only one squeaky rubber ball, or one plastic donut, or one whatever, then that is the toy I want. Unfortunately, that is also the toy that everyone else wants. And even if they don't want it, as soon as I start to play with it, they *will* want it. The desirability of a toy is greatly increased if another dog is playing with it. So if you are lucky enough to get the cool toy, you better be prepared to guard it or it will get stoled.

Note that I do not, nor will I ever, advocate aggression for the sake of a toy. Violence is never the answer. But being alert, adopting a defensive posture, and learning some evasive techniques will defi-

---

1 Author's note: Not having a thumb, I'm not exactly sure what this means, but my person insists that it is a real saying and that it is appropriate here.
2 Author's note: Gloppishness? Gloppitude?

nitely help you keep the toy you want. If and when it does get stoled, no worries; you just have to learn to steal it back.

On a side note: at the park, as at home, the toy I choose to play with is The Toy I Choose To Play With. Which is to say, if we are playing with the blue rubbery ball, don't suddenly decide to throw the green tennis ball, because I will not chase it. I like to call this the Integrity of the Ball. Once a ball has been chosen, a commitment has been made. I will stay with my ball and chase no other. Until I do. And then it's time to play with that one, and no other. And let's be clear: only I am authorized to make that decision.

Now, back to that stealing thing. You may have noticed certain dogs at the park with a predilection for thievery. For example, it is a well-known fact that Beagles are highly skilled kleptodogs. I like Beagles as much as the next gal, but let's face it, they will steal your toy as soon as look at it. When dealing with these and other kleptodogs, it is necessary to come up with diversionary tactics if you wish to reclaim what they stole.

With less sophisticated kleptodogs, like Boxers and Bulldogs, it may suffice to simply stalk them once they have stolen your ball. They may not realize they took someone else's toy, or they may not respect the Integrity of the Ball the same way you do. Often the simple act of following them will alert them to the fact that they have misappropriated property, and they will willingly relinquish it.

But if you are dealing with a hardened criminal thieving Beagle kleptodog, you're going to have to work harder than that. You have to out-klever the klepto. Always remember: you are smarter than they are! Typical kleptodogs are bold, but woefully linear in their thinking. Nuance is lost on them. Their inner dogalogue must go something like this: "Toy. Dog playing with toy. I want toy. Toy toy *toy*! Get toy now! Got toy. Now what?"

This lack of subtlety is a bit pathetic, really, but it's good for you and me. It is the key to the downfall of the kleptodog.

So here's what you do:

First of all, *you have to let them get the toy*. I know, this seems counterintuitive, but trust me. When they grab your toy, you can protest a little, you know, to make it look good. But don't put up a real fight. That's what they expect you to do, and you will lose. They may not have a clue what to do with that toy once they've stoled it, but nonetheless, they will guard it with all they've got.

So, let them think they won. This gives them a false sense of security and puts them off their guard. Then, and only then, you proceed to step two.

Step two is diversion. Take a look around you. What's going on? Are there dogs wrestling? Chasing each other? Chasing a different toy? Join them. While klepto is gloating in his victory, show him you've moved on and you are having an even better time than you were before. His focus will be split between the toy he stoled and the fun he could be having by joining the chase or stealing yet another toy.

As I've indicated earlier, kleptos aren't good at splitting their focus. They can't handle it for too long, and they will almost always go for the new game, leaving your toy behind and unguarded. You can stroll back at your leisure and reclaim it. You can even complete your new game first, if you are enjoying it. The klepto will forget about your toy as soon as he leaves it.

Okay, you say, but what if there's nothing going on around you? Not to worry. You can apply diversionary tactics all by yourself. Sometimes I just do that anyway, because it's so much fun watching the klepto trying to figure out what happened afterwards!

So here's the plan: run around the klepto. A lot. Bark at him. Run toward him, stick your butt in the air, wag your body, and bark like mad. This is the universal dog sign for "Chase me!" For most kleptodogs, the chase is irresistible and will decisively trump the stoled toy for entertainment value. The toy, remember, has already served its purpose; it is passé.[3]

When the klepto chases you, as I guarantee he will, you let him chase you for a moment—and then you spin and dart back the other way and swoop in and grab the toy! *Ha!* Chase my dust, kleptodog! With any luck, your chasing activity will attract others to join in, in which case klepto will become occupied with them and leave you to play with your toy in peace. Worst case, he steals it again, and you steal it back again the same way. He will fall for it again. Every time. Seriously.

---

3 Author's note: Since my name is Belle (French for beautiful), I thought it would be fitting to learn a few French words. For those of you who are not familiar with this language: "It is passé" basically means, "That is *so* five minutes ago!"

MUD IS A MANY
SPLENDORED THING

If there is one thing that every dog understands that every people does not, it is mud.[1] Mud is one of those areas where we have to agree to disagree with our human counterparts. I am not sure why they don't get the incredible beauty of this wondrous substance which is, to our kind, so obvious. Or, as I like to put it, as clear as mud!

First and foremost, mud is slimy! I've already mentioned the superiority of slimy tennis balls. Well, the slimiest ball in the world can't compare to the delicious sliminess of a good mud puddle. It is the holy grail of slimitude.

I've often noticed that people don't share the same reverence for slime that we do. In fact, they seem to avoid slime. Go figure! No matter how hard I try to illustrate that there is nothing quite so en-

---

1 Author's note: There are, in fact, many things that we understand and they do not. I'm using a bit of poetic license here. I'm not sure where you get these poetic licenses, but I'm guessing maybe the same place we got my dog license? Note to self: check on this.

joyable as a good roll in a mud puddle, they resolutely refuse to try it, and they get quite huffy when I do it. If any of you have managed to convince a people otherwise, please tell me how you did this!

On a related note, I once thought I saw something on that box with the flashing pictures about something called mud wrestling. I'm not sure what this is, exactly, but it looked like it involved peoples voluntarily getting into a big vat of mud and splashing around. I am hoping to find out more about this and encourage my person to take up this remarkable activity. I wonder if there's a place where dogs can do this? Maybe dogs and people together? I'm gonna Google[2] this later. Maybe if I leave it up on the screen, my person will get a clue.

So other than sliminess, what are the great benefits of mud? Well, for one thing, it's cool! No, I don't mean cool like "Dude, that's cool." I mean thermally cool. On a sweltering day there is nothing like a dip in the mud to cool you off. I like to roll around on my back, then sprawl out on my stomach and put my legs straight back so I'm totally flat on the ground. This maximizes the surface area of stomach that is exposed to the mud. It's very scientific. Also, sometimes I crawl forward a tad and re-sprawl. This is not scientific, but it is fun and it really gets a good coat of mud onto the fur.

A great place to do this is right by the water bowls at the dog park. Even on a roasting day where the ground is all dry, you can find mud by the water bowls! You see, I have determined, through empirical evidence, that water plus dirt equals mud. Therefore, when water

---

2 Author's note: While it is true that opposable thumbs help with typing, a paw suffices when it comes to pointing and clicking. You just have to tap the mouse. Why they call it a mouse I'm not sure, 'cause it certainly doesn't smell like a mouse. But those peoples have their own kind of logic about these things.

sloshes over the edge of the bowl, or when a people dumps out old water and refreshes the beverage supply, guess what? You get *mud*! I love science.

The first couple of times you do this, you will likely go un-challenged and have a great full-body roll. Unfortunately, I found that my person, while not as scientifically ept as I am, is not entirely inept. Eventually she figured out the water plus dirt thing, and since then it's been much harder to get away with this. As I mentioned before, peoples don't understand the value of mud. Now she watches me very closely when I go to get a drink. If she suspects mudding in-tent, she unceremoniously chases me away, saying, "Don't even think about it." Are you kidding? Of course I'm thinking about it. I dream about it.

So you have to choose your mudding moments carefully. Be aware of those times when your person is distracted, perhaps petting another dog or retrieving the ball you accidentally on purpose left out in the middle of the field (use this sparingly: they will catch on if they come back to a muddy dog every time).

I also recommend the art of the face rub. This is quicker to achieve than the full body rub, so it is harder for your person to stop you. Just stick your head down and slide one side of your face right through that glorious mud puddle. Rub it in good and hard, from the top of your head to the bottom of your ear; and then, if you have time, do the other side. You get all the benefits—the coolness, the sliminess, and that yummy mud smell right up close to your nose—and you can get good and slimed in just a few seconds. It's the most bang for your buck, so to speak, in the mudding world.

If you pay attention, you can develop a sort of radar for mud. I encourage you to develop this skill, because I find that peoples do not have it. This gives you the advantage—if you know there is mud twenty feet ahead, and your person has no idea, then you have a great shot at getting a full body roll in before they know what happened.

Don't get me wrong, your person will be annoyed. But they will also be impressed by your uncanny mud radaring, and the scolding will be tempered by a grudging admiration for your skill.

There is one problem I have not been able to overcome when it comes to mudding. This is the fact that after the mudding always comes the bath. I have racked my brains to come up with a way around this, but I have to admit, I am stumped. Every time I get good and muddy, I get doused, soaped, and doused again. I object to this on so many levels, not the least of which is, I worked hard for that mud! How come I don't get to keep it?

Here's my feeling on the bath: blah! Water is for drinking, not for being in. And hey, let's face it, the wet look is not flattering for me.[3]

I've tried to avoid baths by hiding under the furniture, only to have the furniture moved from over me. I've tried squirming, whining, shaking, and looking pathetic, but to no avail. The bath always comes. My person says I don't understand cause and effect. That's not true, I get it: roll in the mud, you get the bath. But what she doesn't understand is, sometimes it's just plain worth it.

---

3 Translator's note: I have never been able to figure out why Belle will jump over, walk around, or run away from a puddle of clean water when she will voluntarily and gleefully roll around in a puddle of mud. I mean, they're both wet, right? She tells me I don't understand mudding nuance.

WHAT HAPPENS AT
THE DOG PARK . . .

Everybody needs a place where they can just let it all hang out, so to speak, and for a dog, that place is unquestionably the dog park. This is the magical spot where you can really let your inner dog shine. All that stuff that you cannot get away with indoors is pretty much expected here. My person took me to a Passover seder once, and they asked the question, "Why is this night different from all other nights?" Well, the dog park is kind of like that. So let's examine the question, "Why is this place different from all other places?"

Most notably, there are no leashes at the dog park. We are free to roam, explore, run, and play. We can go wherever we choose, and do whatever we choose—roll in it, pee on it, chew on it . . . it's all okay!

Anywhere else, we are expected to promptly obey all commands. But at the park, peoples know we're distracted, and if we don't answer right away when they call, we're not likely to get in trouble. It's the perfect place to use what I like to call "selective hearing."

Selective hearing means that you ignore certain things while responding to others. You have to be wise in practicing this: you know when your person means business. But if they are halfheartedly calling you while you're sniffing out a gopher, or they feebly suggest you stop digging a particularly glorious hole, you might just happen not to hear them.

Sometimes you may not be sure how urgent your person's request is. In this case, you might continue what you are doing, but raise up an ear. Basically you are saying, "I heard you; I'm busy." Don't try this at home, but at the park, it's perfectly acceptable.

Normally, we are supposed to be invited before we go up and lick someone. But at the dog park, no one objects to this behavior. In fact, they think it's cute. I once snuck up stealthily on a woman from behind and zapped a good lick on her face before she knew what was coming. She thought it was hilarious! If I tried that in another locale, I'd probably get a stern talking-to from my person. But not here, oh no! Here everything's fair game.

In a similar vein, it is generally considered bad form to jump up on people. But part of the reason we go to the park is to get exercise . . . and, you can't deny, jumping is exercise. You have to choose carefully: don't jump on a small child or an elderly person, because you could knock them over. But the average person will not have a problem with a little jumping.

One Border Collie I know is an amazing jumper. She has perfected the art of face launching. People don't realize how much skill this takes. You need excellent aim, a strong, quick jump, and the ability to hide your intentions until the last possible second. This dog's technique is flawless: she stands on her hind legs, looking up into the person's face. She gives a couple of calm, quiet face licks, lulling them into a sense of affectionate security. Then *presto*—she launches herself straight up, hitting them square on the face with her nose. Sometimes she even sticks out her tongue and combines the face launch with a face lick. It's a thing of beauty.

The face launch is not for everyone: personally, I prefer a gentler touch, standing up and leaning on a person rather than jumping on them. But for those who feel a need to jump, the dog park is absolutely the place to do it.

Indoors, we are generally not encouraged to bark unless there's an intruder outside. Perhaps you've heard the term "indoor voice"? That's what peoples say when they want us to be quiet. Use your "indoor voice." I have given up trying to explain that I have only one voice, and it is loud. They don't accept this kind of reasoning.

At the park, there is no need to worry about your indoor voice. You can say what you mean, and say it as loud as you want. Bark to encourage a dog to chase you, or to tell it to leave you alone. Bark at the people jogging on the other side of the fence. Howl at the moon. Yap at the new dog to welcome him to the park. This is your forum. Get on your soapbox[1] and bark for all you're worth.

My person has requested that I address one particular sub-

---

1 Author's note: My person tells me that people stand on these when they make speeches. Not being a fan of the bath, I don't know why anyone would have a big box of soap in the first place.

ject here: With all the barking, running, and wrestling that goes on at the park, how do you, as a person, know when dogs are playing and when they are fighting?

I was a little surprised by this question, because it's perfectly clear to us what we are doing. But I realize that not all peoples speak Dog as well as mine does. So I will address this question for the benefit of the dog-speak challenged.

First: the sounds. There is a specific, high-pitched, squealy sound that dogs make when they are hurt or truly scared. It's very distinctive, and if you hear it, you know there is something wrong.

Other sounds are trickier. Barking may alarm you, but usually we are just having a conversation. "Chase me," "I don't want to chase you," "Chase me," "Leave me alone," "*Chase me!*" is a typical example of a dog park barking match.

Growling is perhaps the most difficult of all for humans to interpret. It can, in certain circumstances, be a warning of impending doom. It is a good idea for peoples to closely monitor any growling behavior that seems out of the ordinary, in case it escalates into fighting. In which case, squealing will soon follow.

The growl, however, is not always "fightin' words." I, for one, am a big growler when I play. I might growl when I dive after a ball, and I definitely growl when I am chasing another dog. It's just part of the game. It makes me feel fierce.

Ultimately, peoples should monitor all growling but try not to jump to conclusions. Get to know your dog and how to tell a "play growl" from the real deal. Check the rest of our body language for signs of play (slack mouth, relaxed ears, relaxed and wagging tail, front end down and butt in the air) or aggression (bared teeth, ears back, rigid tail, body leaning forward and ready to lunge). Err on the side of caution, to be sure, but base your decision to intervene on the whole picture, not just a single growl.

There is one other fail-safe way to evaluate a wrestling match for trouble: Which dog is on top? If a Husky is pinning a Chihuahua,[2] there may be reason to intervene. But if a Yorkie is perched, growling, atop a Doberman who has rolled over on his back, I'm gonna say that they are playing.

Don't get me wrong: in matters of dog aggression, size doesn't matter. I know several incredibly sweet Great Danes, and I've also met purse dogs who would love nothing more than to take a bite out of everyone they meet. But generally speaking, when the snack-sized dog is dominating the big bad beast, there is no need to worry.

Now, back to park etiquette: there is one particular type of behavior that peoples consider completely unacceptable, even at the dog park. I think you know of what I speak, but just in case, let me be blunt: there is no humping at the dog park.

As far as I can tell, this is the first commandment of dog behavior: Thou shalt not hump. Thou shalt especially not hump in public. Thou shalt not hump thy neighbor's wife, thy neighbor's leg, or thy neighbor's Jack Russell Terrier. And, let there be no mistake: Thou shalt not hump at the dog park.

People seem to think there is something unseemly or dirty

---

2 Author's note: I know, I know, who could blame him?

about the act of humping. You and I know, of course, that generally it has nothing to do with sex. I mean, most of us don't have the . . . equipment . . . anymore that we would need in order to reproduce.[3]

Humping, for the most part in civilized dog society, is about dominance. It's instinct, plain and simple. But I've learned that since peoples don't use it this way, they have a hard time separating the action from the intention, if you get my drift.

On a separate yet related note, I find it interesting that people sometimes describe their own promiscuous males as "dogs." It seems to me that we are getting a bad rap here. People, next time you call your cheating spouse a "dog," please take a moment to stop and think: "Is this really fair to dogs?"

I got humping out of my system at an early age. For a couple of weeks, when I was four months old, I experimented with a particularly nice pink pillow. I admit, I enjoyed myself. More importantly, at that point in time I really needed an outlet to express myself as I established my own identity. My person understood and agreed that I was allowed to dominate that pillow. And, let me tell you, I dominated the heck out of it.

Then I got over it.

Apparently, it doesn't work this way for all dogs. And that's why every dog park has its own version of what I like to call "the Mad Humper." I'm sure you've seen it: the one dog whose idea of a

---

3 Author's note: If you don't know what I mean, there is a chance you still have it. But it is also possible that certain information has been withheld from you. If you are not sure, you might want to have a talk with your person. Ask them what wearing that cone on your head when you were six months old was all about. And no, it was not a fashion statement.

fun day at the park is nothing more or less than humping every dog in sight. No amount of scolding will deter the Mad Humper from his quest. No degree of bribery will convince the Mad Humper to give it up. And no matter how many dogs the Mad Humper humps, he will never be satisfied.

Sometimes the Mad Humper will choose one particular dog to dominate for the day. In that situation, he will continue to seek out this pup and mount it again and again. Each time, he will be pulled off by an embarrassed and increasingly irate person. And each time, he will do it again. Guaranteed.

I can only surmise that these Mad Humpers have never played a proper game of fetch. If they had any idea of the excitement, the joy, the unadulterated bliss of chasing a ball at breakneck speed across a grassy field, they would realize that their energy is entirely misdirected.

Some would say that this would be substituting one addiction for another. To these people I say, "So what?" You have your cup of coffee every morning, don't you? And anyway, I don't need the ball, I just like it. A lot. I can stop anytime I want to. Anytime! I—

My person is very proud of herself right now. She thinks because she just threw the ball and I dropped everything and chased it, she has proven a point. But I am in control. There is—

Darn it! Okay, maybe I have a problem. But I'm okay with that. Now, stop laughing, and throw the ball!

WORKING THE CROWD

I'd like to broaden the scope of our discussion now, beyond the park, to cover pretty much any social situation in which you find yourself. For example, your person may have guests at your place of livingness. You may be walking down a busy street. Or you may be sitting at an outdoor coffee shop, or some such place. Whatever the situation, if you know how to work the crowd, you'll get a lot more attention and have a lot more fun.

Crowd-working tip 1: Judge the LP.

Each group of people, and each person within that group, will have a different degree of dog receptiveness. Your job is to accurately judge the dynamic of the group and determine your best chance for getting attention. I call this judging the LP (Licking Potential). If you're not into licking faces, then substitute whatever words work for you. Loving Potential, perhaps. Whatever bakes your biscuit.

Let me use for an example the outdoor seating area of a Starbucks, which is one of my favorite places to work the crowd.

So, the first thing you have to do is check out the people who are already seated, enjoying their caffeinated beverage of choice. Some will actively avoid you by moving away or pointedly looking in another direction. Forget about it; these are probably Cat People, and your efforts are better used elsewhere.

Some will ignore you. That may or may not be a rejection. File it in the category of more research needed; try again later.

Then there are the ones who will engage you, making eye contact, reaching out a hand, or speaking to you. These are your gold mine. Very high LP here.

In order to get an accurate LP reading, you have to approach each table in the right way. I know it's tempting to just run up and jump on them, but I counsel you against this course of action. Crowd working requires much more finesse.

LP is not set in stone. You must identify where the highest LP is, and cultivate it with the best dog behavior (according to people standards) that you can. Let me repeat: *according to people standards.* This is an essential point to remember, because people standards of good behavior tend to be different from dog standards of good behavior. If you're not sure what I mean, I refer you to the last chapter's discussion of humping.

So the question becomes, how do you properly approach a people? You need an invitation, so how do you get it? This may seem like a daunting task, but the key thing to remember is this: you are cute. Use it. Shamelessly.

When you approach a new person, you need to be excited but not frenetic. Wagging your tail is good. Smiling is great. Gazing into their eyes with a look that says, "I am so glad to see you!" is fantastic. Note: the look needs to be genuine and should convey a sense of longing but not desperation. Desperate is not cute. It will not get your belly rubbed.

Think of yourself as the welcome wagon. Every time a new person arrives, it is your job to greet them like a long-lost friend. Your internal dogalogue should be something like, "Oh, my goodness! It is you! I was hoping you'd be here today—I've missed you so much! Let me give you lots of love and face licks!"

So now you're thinking, "But I've never met this person before. How can I miss them?" Here's the thing: it doesn't matter! You miss them. "But they know they haven't met me," you say. "They won't believe I miss them." You have to trust me on this: they *will*. If you really, really miss them, they will believe!

See, if you miss them, then you're already friends. If you miss them, obviously you love them. You don't have to waste time or energy professing your love; it's a given. And remember, you are not begging for adoration or attention. You are simply thrilled for the opportunity to shower affection on this wonderful person.

Next time you find yourself in a social situation, try this exercise. Greet a new person by approaching them eagerly but respectfully. If you are on a leash, strain against it lightly—enough so that you are leaning forward toward the new person, but not so much that you are ripping the arm off of your person. You want to be enthusiastic here, not barbaric.

While you are leaning—and this is key!—you need to make direct eye contact with the person you are trying to meet. Make your eyes as big as you can, and gaze into theirs as deeply as you can. All the while think to yourself, "Hi! I missed you! I'm so happy to see you! My day is complete because I have seen you!" Think this as loud as you can, so they can hear you.

A slightly open mouth and a little panting never hurt anyone. Relax your jaw, wag your tail, and if you have ears that pop up, you might try popping them. Oh, and if you are able to stand up on two legs, I highly encourage it; people really like this.

I am going to share with you my signature[1] move: the stand-and-lean. This is the civilized dog's answer to jumping up on peoples. Instead of pouncing, you simply stand up—gracefully—and gently rest your paw on the person to help maintain your balance.

I must stress the concepts of grace and gentleness here. You are not flinging yourself up and knocking into the person on your way back down. You are not clinging to them for support. You are simply standing straight up and then lightly leaning, exerting as little pressure as you can. You are more than welcome to try this on your own, but I beg you not to butcher the move and say you learned it from me. I have a reputation to maintain.

Standing on two legs has become second nature to me, and I must say I have refined it to an art form. I discovered as a puppy that

---

1 Author's note: A signature, I am told, is a mark people make to show their identity, like a paw print. Or, for male dogs, like peeing on stuff.

I could do it, and I was rewarded with oohing and aahing and petting and a biscuit. Suffice it to say, I decided to repeat the experience.

Standing up has other benefits, too. It gets you closer to the face you are trying to lick. It allows easy access for belly rubbing. And when a bunch of people are standing around talking, a good stand-and-lean gets you in on the action! You may not follow the whole conversation, but I guarantee you that at least one of those people will scratch your ear and rub your belly.

One more tip: when you are out walking, and a car pulls up and stops at the curb next to you, chances are a person is going to get out of that car in a few seconds. I recommend standing up on two legs and staring directly at the person through the window of the car. Remember to do everything else I told you: relax, smile, make eye contact, and miss that person with all you've got! At least half of the time, this will result in the person coming over to pet you when they get out of the car.

For those of you that are balance challenged, I encourage you to come up with signature moves of your own that are compatible with your body type. Instead of the stand-and-lean, you can try the sit-and-lean, where you sit on or near their foot and lean on their leg. I can't promise the same results—peoples really dig the standing thing—but the sit-and-lean is a classic and never goes out of style. If you discover something else that works, I'd love to hear about it!

Always remember: *there are no strangers.* The world is your friend! If you acknowledge this simple truth, own it, and live by its wisdom, you will be way ahead of the pack!

Crowd-working tip 2: Drop the ball.

Now, there are times when face licking is not uppermost in your mind. Perhaps your tongue is tired, perhaps you have grown bored of face licking, or perhaps you have sufficiently licked all available faces.[2]

Sometimes I am in licking mode, and sometimes I am in playing mode. If I am in playing mode, I am going to want to encourage nearby peoples to play with me, because let's face it, a ball is pretty boring if no one is throwing it. Except if you are pulling all the fuzz off with your teeth. That's pretty fun. But I digress.

I have found that the best way to get a person to throw a ball is the bring-and-drop. It sounds very simple, and it is, but there are ways to add your own personal touches and increase your fetching enjoyment.

There is absolutely no subtlety in the properly executed bring-and-drop. You need to walk directly up to the person with ball in mouth and drop it in front of them with a resounding thud.[3] The best way to do this is to raise your head slightly with the ball still in your mouth, and then half drop, half fling it onto the ground. It may take a little practice because you don't want the ball to bounce or roll away; a well-dropped ball will stay exactly where you put it.

But guess what? When the ball hits the floor, you're not done

---

2 Author's note: I have never personally experienced any of these things, but I suppose it is possible for a tongue to get tired or to get bored of licking. As for sufficiently licking all available faces, well, I would argue that there is always another face, and a licker's work is never done. But that's just my opinion.
3 Author's note: If you are indoors and on carpeting, the thud will be less impressive, but the same effect can be achieved as long as you drop the ball with attitude.

yet! And this is where some dogs, if you'll pardon the expression, drop the ball on dropping the ball! The drop is just the first step in a complex social interaction, hopefully resulting in a mutually fulfilling play session.

Again, eye contact is key: you are inviting this person to play a game with you. Looking directly into their eyes, with an eager, anticipatory expression on your face, is how you do this. You are not just asking to play a game—the game has already started, and you are anxiously awaiting their first move.

There is a difference between gazing eagerly and staring maniacally. The former will get you a game of fetch. The latter will get you a shrink and doggie Prozac. Every so often, break eye contact to look at the ball, then look at the face. The ball, the face. Ball, face. This way you are clearly asking for what you want, and you don't turn into psycho-stare-contest-never-blinking dog. 'Cause let's face it, that dog is weird.

It helps to take a couple of steps backward after you drop the ball, so they know you are ready to play. I like to put one paw in the air, like a pointer, to show that I am prepared for the throw. You may have another method; I know a Border Collie who lies down in a crouching position ready to spring when his Frisbee flies. Find your favorite move, then stick with it.

So, what if you have perfectly executed the bring-and-drop, and the person does not immediately throw the ball? Relax, all is not lost. Sometimes peoples get a little rusty on their training and need a reminder or some extra encouragement to get with the program.

First, just repeat the bring-and-drop. Pick up the ball again, drop it, and resume eager (not manic) staring. You sometimes need to do this two or three times before the person grasps the concept. You can enhance the message by dropping it closer to them each time. If they are sitting down, you might place the ball next to them or right on their lap. Always remember: make it as easy as possible for them to give you what you want.

If that still doesn't work, you might want to add some auditory signals. Pathetic whimpering, a skill that most of us master by the age of four months, can be quite useful here. To change things up, I sometimes like to use the teeth snap. Nothing threatening here, just a quick click of the jaw in the direction of the ball, followed by an eager gaze into the person's eyes. Finally, you might try a playful growl, but I caution you: you need to practice your growly sounds and train your person to know which ones mean "let's play" and which ones mean business. Otherwise, you will get in trouble.

I recommend that you spend some time playing growly tug-of-war, growly wrestling, and growly keep-away with your person, to get them used to the concept of play-growling. Do not full-on play-growl at them until they have completed this training, or you will once again be risking the shrink and the doggie Prozac.

Crowd-working tip 3: Kids.

There will be times when you find yourself face-to-face with one or more kids. No doubt you have experienced these already at some point, and you may have formed your own opinion of these beings. I can only share with you my personal experiences, preferences, and observations.

First of all, let's talk about babies. My person tells me that these beings are actually peoples, just littler. As a rule, my person does not lie to me, so I guess it's true . . . although I do not see the resemblance. I have nothing against babies, I just don't understand them. They don't walk, they don't play, they cannot throw a ball, and they scream. What, then, is their purpose? Best to ignore these critters.

When they get a little older, they start to appear more personesque. Not entirely as cool as a full-sized people, but closer. I guess what I'm saying is this: until it can throw a ball, it's pretty much useless to me. Once it can do that, it is officially, by my definition, a person.

Like any puppy, a kid needs to be trained. Their parents are the ones who do this, but we dogs can help by reinforcing the behavior we like. Give them a kiss when they pat you on the head. Gently remove your tail from their grabbing hand and rub your side against them instead. Roll over on your back to show how much you love belly rubs. They want to make you happy; you just have to show them the correct way to do it.

The best thing about kids is their enthusiasm. They show pure, unabashed love and joy, much like dogs do. They are honest—what you see is what you get. I like that in a people.

A while ago my person decided I was certifiable.[4] Since then,

---

4 Translator's note: Actually, I've always known Belle was certifiable, but that's beside the point. What she means here is that we both trained and took a test to become a certified therapy dog and handler. We volunteered as a team at various locations in the Los Angeles area, often visiting children.

I've spent lots of time with big groups of kids. There is nothing quite like walking into a room full of kids who want nothing more than to love on you. All that attention, and all the faces are within easy licking range! How cool is that? But the best part is I can feel how happy they are, and that makes me happy. If you think you are certifiable, you might want to try therapy dogging!

Crowd-working tip 4: The art of the Pity Lick.

So, how do you balance your desire to meet and greet new peoples with the need to show love and devotion to your own person above all others? This is a tricky problem, but not an unsolvable one.

Now, there are dogs who show loyalty and affection only to their own people and want nothing to do with anyone else. They also tend to get bent out of shape if another dog gets too close to their person. If you fall into this category, you might want to skip the rest of this chapter. Or read on, and you might learn something. I'm just saying.

My person is the bestest person in the world, and I do not hesitate to tell her that on a regular basis. But I am by nature a very social dog, and when we are out and about, I want to meet other people too. And let's face it, I lick my person all the time. When we're out, I want to lick that person . . . and that one . . . and those ones over there!

My person and I came to an understanding quite some time ago: she is allowed to pet other dogs, and I am allowed to lick other faces. We are both secure enough in our relationship not to be threatened by this. After all, we both know who is going home together at the end of the day.

That being said, there are times when you want to tell your person, "I love you the best." I suggest using the Pity Lick. Basically, when you've been off licking other people for a while, and your person is standing there watching you from afar, take a moment and run over to her and give a lick or two. That's all it takes! Message delivered, and you are now free to go back and find more faces.

I should emphasize here that the Pity Lick is no different in feeling or intent than any other lick; it is simply the situation that defines it. The Pity Lick is quicker than the average face lick, but no less genuine. Therein lies the challenge: you must convey the same amount of affection in a shorter amount of time.

Really, it isn't that hard. All I have to do is look into my person's face, and I am overwhelmed with feelings of love. This is what I am thinking of when I go in for the lick, Pity or otherwise. So whether I lick her for an hour, a minute, or a second, I am confident that my message is conveyed.[5]

If you are able to perfect the art of the Pity Lick and incorporate it into your daily life, you will be well-equipped to enjoy fulfilling emotional relationships not only with your own person, but also with all other peoples. And really, that's what being a dog is all about.

---

5 Translator's note: It is.

WAS I NOT SUPPOSED
TO DO THAT?

So we have covered many types of dog-people interactions, in a variety of settings, and everything is good. You are now in a mature, mutually fulfilling relationship with your person and communication between the two of you has never been better! In fact, it is so good that you understand each other perfectly at all times and there is absolutely no conflict whatsoever. Life is a bowl of biscuits.

Yeah, right.

No matter how good your relationship is, there will be moments when something goes wrong. One of you (generally the canine one) does something that has been expressly forbidden. And someone (you know of whom I speak) is in trouble. How do you handle these situations?

Maybe you remember the first time you chewed up your person's manila blahblah,[1] or peed on her bed,[2] or otherwise mutilated some prized item. Most likely, your person was not too pleased. But, if she is a cool people, like mine, she understood that you meant no harm; you simply did not know that this behavior was unacceptable. Hopefully, at this point, she patiently taught you not to do it again.

Now let me ask you this: did you do it again?

If you answered "no," you're not fooling anyone but yourself. I know as well as the next dog that sometimes the urge to misbehave is irresistible. While true remorse and time are the only things that really fix one of these gaffes, there are a few techniques you might try when faced with the wrath of your person.

Technique 1: Play dumb.

Perhaps the simplest and most instinctive of all the techniques, the first thing you might try is to play dumb. Remember how the first time you did something wrong, you were not punished so much as corrected? Well, it follows that if you didn't know what you did was wrong this time, you should not be punished for it either!

So your goal here is to convey one of three messages: 1–that you were never told not to do what you just did; 2–that you may have been told, but you don't remember; or 3–that you were told, but you just did not understand.

It is up to you to decide which is the most appropriate strategy. If you have only been told something once, it may be plausible

---

1 Translator's note: I think she means Manolo Blahnik here. And no, I don't own any. Maybe there was a rerun of *Sex and the City* on one night. I don't know where she gets some of this stuff.

2 Author's note: I must stress that I have never done this; I think it's disgusting. But I have heard that some dogs actually do this sort of thing, so I am including it as an example for the hygienically challenged among my readers. To whom I say, stop it!

that you think you weren't told at all. If you were told a couple of times, maybe you can pull off the "I forgot!" scenario. If you've been told ten, fifty, or a hundred times, you'd better stick with "I didn't understand what you meant." But be careful, because if you do this too many times, your person won't buy it—or worse, they'll think you're really that stupid.

Whichever approach you choose, the first thing you have to do is not look guilty when they walk in the door. Bowing your head, cowering in the corner, or putting a pathetic expression on your face are all sure signs of guilt—and will completely undermine your defense. If you didn't know you were bad, why would you feel guilty?

You should approach your person in a relaxed, joyful manner, just like you would if you hadn't knocked over the garbage can. You might bring them a toy to show you are ready to play. You can wag your tail and dance around to show how happy you are to see them. Not afraid, not apprehensive, and not ashamed. Happy!

There will come a moment during your happy dance when your person will stop you and explain that you did something wrong. She might pick up a shredded piece of book and hold it in front of your face. She might yell at you, ignore you, or just give you a long, sad, disappointed look.

This is where you must convey the idea that you had no idea whatsoever that you misbehaved at all! It's news to you, and you are dismayed to hear it. Most of all, you want to know what you did because you would never want to do it again. This is the proper time to look ashamed. Surprised, ashamed, and sorry.

Which leads to the apology. You owe your person a genuine apology, complete with face licking and whatever else you can think of to show how much you love her. You are expressing your remorse and your determination to do better in the future.

If you have carried out this defense correctly, your person will forgive you and return the affection. She will give you the benefit of the doubt and chalk it up to a learning experience.

Technique 2: Look cute.

Do I really have to explain this? It's one of the basic tools in the dog arsenal: you are cute. Any dog worth the name knows this and is not afraid to use it to their best advantage.

Now, being cute only goes so far. You need to know your limits. If all you did was rip up the Sunday *Times*, a cute look and pathetic puppy dog eyes will go a long way toward getting you off the hook. But if you ate the living room couch, smashed the good crystal, or gnawed the legs off of the dining room table, well, you might be looking at a more comprehensive repentance process.

Here's something interesting I have learned over the years: peoples place values on objects, and their values aren't the same as ours. But knowing their value system is the key to understanding how much trouble you are in for whatever it is that you did.

For me, the Sunday *Times* is an object that is really cool for shredding. But for my person, it is something to look at, write in, and talk about. For both of us, the couch is something comfy to sit on—but for me, it is also something filled with highly pullout-able stuffing. For her, not so much. Peoples really don't like it when you do that.[3]

You may remember my system for determining whether an object is good: is it fetchable, is it chewable, is it lickable? Well, peoples have a different set of criteria, which, from my experience, go something like this: is it valuable, is it useful, is it replaceable?

Valuable stuff costs a lot of money, that green paper stuff—which, incidentally, is another thing they do not like us to shred.[4] Valuable things include couches and other furniture, the aforementioned green paper, and various other objects; unfortunately, there is not really any way for us dogs to know what is valuable except to get punished for destroying it. One you have done it, you will know. Being cute will help you with this, but you will have to work it for all it's worth. I recommend adding a large dose of pathetic to the basic cute. I won't go into more detail because I know that you know what I'm talking about.

Useful items are anything that your person intends to read, listen to, give to someone else, or otherwise use in the course of their daily life. They include (again) furniture, books, CDs, credit cards, certain pieces of paper—honestly, I can't explain why some paper is okay to shred and some is not, but I can definitely tell you that some of it is not okay! Cuteness may help you here, but you'd better be *really* cute.

Items that are irreplaceable are the worst things to destroy; you will get in the most trouble, and looking cute will not help you at

---

3 Author's note: I speak from experience on this one.
4 Author's note: Yes, I speak from experience on this one too. What's your point?

all. The really frustrating thing is that it's impossible for us to know what is replaceable and what is not. I mean, come on! How could I know that something has "sentimental value" for my person? I don't even know what "sentimental value" is!

Irreplaceable items can be misleading too, because quite often our peoples don't use them, look at them, or even touch them very often. So it seems to us that they are simply random, unuseful items. I mean, if you put something on a shelf, and don't play with it for, like, two years, I figure you probably don't like it that much. I play with my toys every day!

If you have the unfortunate experience of destroying something irreplaceable, I wish you the best of luck—you will need it. Like I said, being cute won't get you out of this one, but, it will help you in the long run. After a certain amount of time has passed, your person will look at you, and you will give her that sweet, loving gaze that says, "IamsosorryIreallyreallyreallyloveyouIwillneverdoitagain!" And she will forgive you. Not because you are cute, but because she loves you. The cuteness will help her remember that love. Always remember: love conquers all. Even if you ripped up her wedding dress.[5]

Technique 3: Make 'em laugh.

When we're doing something our people don't want us to do, they try to get us to do what they do want us to do. One of the ways they do this is by distracting us with a toy.

A lot of dogs don't realize this is happening. But think about it: How many times have you been involved in some activity—bark-

---

5 Author's note: This is just an example! I highly do not recommend doing this!

ing, whining, digging a hole in the carpet, chewing your own paw—when suddenly, your person appeared and waved your favorite toy in front of your face? What did you do? More likely than not, you forgot what you were doing and played with the toy.

See what they did there? You didn't know it at the time, but now it all starts to make sense, right?

I mention this for two reasons: first of all, because I think it's important to have a good understanding of what is going on in the world around you. It doesn't mean you won't grab the toy the next time this happens. But you'll remember this secret that I'm sharing with you, and you will see the situation in a more complete way.

Secondly, it brings me to the next getting-out-of-trouble technique: making them laugh. This is based on exactly the same principle. Much as your person can distract you from your current activity with a toy, you can distract them from their current frustration by doing something funny. If you do it really well, they might not even realize that you are using their own strategy on them!

"But what can I do?" you may ask. "I am not funny," you say. Yes, you are! Maybe not intentionally, maybe not even consciously, but you are most definitely funny.

Has your person ever laughed when you shook the water off yourself after a bath? Or when you sniffed another dog's butt? Or when you slid across the living room floor while chasing your ball? These events may not have seemed funny to you; they are, after all, normal events in a dog's life. But for a people, they are highly amusing.

I like to dry off completely after a bath. By completely, I mean every drop of water must be *off* of me! In order to do this, I must flop, slide, rub, crawl, and roll on the carpet, the couch, and whatever else is handy until the process is complete. This takes about ten minutes.[6] I always used to wonder why my person watched me, fascinated and laughing hysterically, when I did this. After all, I am 100 percent serious—I mean business! But I gradually realized that she finds this behavior incredibly funny.[7]

So how do I use this information the next time I am in a bind? Well, here's what I've learned. My person likes to laugh, and she does it when she's happy. I am able to make her laugh sometimes, and that also makes her happy. So now that I've identified a specific behavior that makes her laugh, I have an ace in the hole for the next time I am . . . for lack of a better term, in a hole! And it's going to help me climb back out.

For example, if I have ripped up a book, I might start by playing dumb; but if it's the fifth book I've ripped up this week, that ain't gonna fly. So I'll try a new tack: they think it's funny when I flop around like a crazy dog, so I'll fling myself on the floor on my back and roll around a bit. This works on many levels. Exposing my belly is submissive, which suggests an apology. It is also cute. The book is useful, but probably not irreplaceable, so cute might work. And, if you commit fully to the act of flinging yourself down to the ground and flopping for all you're worth, it is funny!

6 Author's note: Okay, I'm pretty dry after five or six, but once I get started, it's hard to stop!
7 Translator's note: It is. I call it "The Afterbath."

I have now distracted the person from the initial displeasure they felt when they walked in the door and saw the book scattered all over the floor. I disarmed them with the pitiful, cute look that said, "Did I do something wrong? I didn't mean to!" From there, I went directly into a tried-and-true comedic routine that is sure to leave them laughing. If they're laughing, they're happy. If they're happy, they're not mad.

Finish out this strategy with a clear submissive pose: roll on your back and invite them to come accept the apology with a little belly rub. Betcha ten biscuits they will!

Technique 4: If all else fails, hide under the couch.

If, after your best efforts at techniques 1 through 3, your person is still mad, then a little cooling down period may be a good idea. This would be a good time to crawl under the couch, the bed, or some other space big enough for you but too small for your person.

Your person will understand from this that you are remorseful, that you know there are consequences for your bad behavior, and that you are ashamed of yourself. They may believe you're under there thinking about what you did. In truth, you're probably just taking a nap, but they don't need to know that. You've conveyed the message with the simple act of slinking off[8] and crawling under the futon.

One dog I knew adapted this strategy quite well to her particular situation. Whenever she misbehaved, her people would make

---

8 Author's note: It is essential that you slink. Your head should be down, in a posture of shame, and you should move slowly, like you are plodding through a pool of molasses. This is one moment when direct eye contact is not appropriate.

her go out to the laundry room and stay there alone for a while. Now, this was a pretty effective punishment, because she really hated sitting in that room alone. But she recognized that this was necessary in order for her people to forgive her. So, when her people were angry, she didn't wait for them to punish her. She took herself to the laundry room.

This is really brilliant. First of all, she knew she was going to the laundry room. That was set in stone. But instead of being dragged in there squirming and whining, she walked in willingly, and thus kept her dignity.

At the same time, she conveyed an understanding of the situation, remorse for her actions, and acceptance of the idea that she deserved to be punished. Her people were most likely impressed by her maturity and intelligence. This helped speed along the process of forgiveness, minimizing the total amount of time spent in the laundry room—which is exactly what our clever dog wanted in the first place! Brilliant.

Remember, as I said at the beginning of this chapter, true remorse and time are the only things that will really right the wrong and repair your relationship. None of these techniques are meant to replace that. But proper use of them, alone or in combination, should help you get through the difficult times.

NEVER LET ON HOW MUCH YOU REALLY KNOW

Dogs are highly intelligent creatures. I state this not because it is big news (being a dog, you already knew you were smart); and I'm not bragging. I'm merely presenting an irrefutable, undeniable fact: dogs are highly intelligent creatures.

If it's so obvious, why mention it at all? Well, you may remember from the last chapter that "playing dumb" is one of the things that can get you out of a troublesome spot. Now, I would never advise a canine to play dumb all the time. First of all, no one would believe you. Secondly, it would tarnish the good name of dogs everywhere.

But just because you're not acting stupid, it doesn't mean you have to reveal the true extent of your own brilliance. I would recommend that you give your person glimpses—quick flashes, if you will—of the genius that you are. But all in all, it is to your advantage to keep some of your wisdom to yourself. It gives you an element of control while you test the boundaries of your relationship with your person. I encourage you to consider the following tips as you undergo this process.

Tip 1: People-speak: not as hard as you'd think.

If you're like me, the first time you heard people-speak, you were probably pretty confused. All these sounds were coming your way, and some of them seemed to be directed to you, but what on earth did they mean? You were fluent in the language of barks, whines, and growls, but not in this strange dialect. You knew, though, that there was meaning there, and you wanted to figure it out.

Maybe you first grasped the concept of your own name. People said it to you all the time, and at some point you realized they were talking to you.[1] You probably learned "sit" shortly after this. After that, things started to become clear much more quickly; once you understood that these sounds were words—and the same word meant the same thing every time—you were well on your way to becoming a great communicator.

Now every dog learns at their own pace, and some are more languagely inclined than others. The most verbally gifted among us may learn more quickly, but I am confident that any dog can grasp the basics of people-speak enough to follow most conversations. I don't always choose to listen, because sometimes I'm just not interested. But if I am listening, I understand. Maybe not every single word, but enough that I get what's going on.

My person had this book once[2] that had drawings in it, and

---

1 I had a few moments where I wasn't sure whether my name was "Belle" or "Nobelle," but that's another matter. Suffice it to say I figured it out, and also learned what "no" meant.
2 Author's note: Okay, I ate the book. But while I shredded it, I saw some of the stuff inside, and it was rather amusing. I almost felt bad about ripping it up. Almost.

there was one about what people say vs. what dogs hear. The person was talking to the dog and what the dog heard was something like, "Blah blah blah Belle, blah blah Belle, blah blah blah blah Belle!"[3]

There is some truth to this representation. While we learn many words, not just our own name, there are a lot of nonsense words in there that all pretty much sound the same. You have to use context, tone, and common sense to fill in the blanks. For example, if we are at the park, and I get distracted in the middle of a game of fetch and come back without my ball, my owner might say something like: "Belle, blah blah, ball, blah blah, over there. Blah blah blah blah, ball!" Judging by the context (I know perfectly well where my ball is) and her posture (she's pointing in the direction of the ball), I can tell that she just said, "Belle, you left your ball all the way over there. Will you please go get your ball!"

See how easy that is? You can apply this logic to most situations and fill in the blanks well enough to understand most of what is said to you and about you. The rest of the stuff they say is pretty boring, and although you could figure it out too, it's probably not worth the effort. Your time might be better spent grooming yourself or digging a hole in the futon.

Here are some common phrases and their rough translations:

"Blah blah blah mud, blah blah bath." (If you roll in the mud, you get a bath.)

"Blah blah bring blah ball, blah blah throw blah blah!" (If you bring me the ball, I will throw it for you!)

---

3 Translator's note: Credit this to a "Far Side" cartoon. The dog's name was actually Ginger, not Belle. Darn, I liked that book.

55

"Blah blah blah hungry dog? Blah blah supper?" (Are you a hungry dog? Would you like some supper?)

"Blah blah blah blah park?[4]" (Do you want to go to the park?)

You get the idea. The key here is to determine whether what is being said is Important to Dog or Not Important to Dog, and adjust your level of attention accordingly.

I've also noticed that sometimes peoples don't say what they mean. For example, let's say I've shredded a book while my person was out. When she comes home and sees the damage, she might ask me, "What did you do?" Now, that's confusing, because clearly she knows exactly what I did. She's looking right at it. What she is really asking me is, "*Why* did you do?" And she is also telling me that she is not pleased with what I did and would prefer that I do not do it again.

How do I get all this meaning out of, "What did you do?" By paying attention to the tone and the rhythm in which it is asked. This is not a simple question, asked in a happy, bouncy tone of voice; rather, it is a statement, given in a low-pitched, drawn-out, scolding voice: "Whaaat. Did. Yoouuuuu. Dooooooooooooooooooo?" The meaning is conveyed not in the words, but in the way in which they are said. Always remember, when interpreting people-speak, words are not everything. If you miss the tone, you miss the point.

A final note about people-speak: it may behoove you to learn how to spell certain words. People assume that we cannot do this, so they sometimes take to spelling things out when they don't want us to understand what they are saying. T-R-E-A-T for treat, P-A-R-K

---

4 Author's note: Fill in whatever word fits here: park, walk, car, play . . .

for park, B-A-T-H for bath, and stuff like that. It's not too hard to figure out which combination of letters stands for which word.

Learning to spell gives you the upper hand as long as you don't let them *know* you can spell. Remember this: you cannot react to the spelled words, no matter how much you want the T-R-E-A-T or how much you don't want the B-A-T-H. If you start drooling or panting or running away, they'll find some other way to communicate when they don't want you to hear. If you keep your cool, they'll be none the wiser and they'll freely spell out all sorts of stuff right in front of you.

Tip 2: Keep 'em guessing.

Peoples love to analyze dog intelligence. They know dogs are smart, and they love to believe that their dog is the smartest of all dogs.[5] But, they also believe that dogs are not as smart as peoples. This is where they are mistaken, and it opens the door for us to have a bit of fun.

Now, it takes a bit of finesse, but what I recommend (and what I myself practice) is to reinforce both of these notions in your people. They must believe that you are brilliant, but that they are more brilliant. They will be proud of your accomplishments, and they will think that certain things are beyond your grasp. When you do something they don't think you can do, they will not only be impressed, they will also question their entire system of smartness analysis. Then you will carefully lull them back into a sense of false superiority.

---

5 Author's note: They are, of course, in denial; *I* am the smartest of all dogkind.

Let me give you an example.

One day we were at the park, enjoying a rousing game of fetch. There were a few other dogs there, also playing fetch with their peoples, all of us relishing the sunlight and luxuriating in the thick, soft grass.[6]

After about twenty tosses of the ball, I got distracted by something and went to investigate. I left the ball where it landed, making note of its location for later retrieval. After checking out the new smell/sound/whatever it was, I returned to my person for some affection and a little break.

My person, as usual, was unnaturally obsessed with the fact that I did not bring back the ball. I believe the conversation went something like this:

"Where's the ball, Belle? I think you forgot something . . . You left the ball way out there! Go get your ball! Get the ball! Get it!"

I ignored her.

"Belle, you know if you don't bring it back, it's not fetch. It's just feh."

I sniffed the grass.

"How many jobs do you have? Just the one, really . . . Bring back the ball."

I rolled over, flopped around in the grass, and then stretched out and made myself comfortable.

It was at about this point that one of the other dogs' peoples

_____

6 Translator's note: I think Belle has been playing with the thesaurus feature on my computer . . .

asked my people, "Does she have any idea what you are saying to her?"

My ears perked up at that, but I did not let on that I was listening.

"No," said my person with a sigh, "she has no idea. I could say that all day long and she wouldn't go out there and get the ball."

That was my cue!

I promptly picked myself up, trotted out to the spot in the middle of the field where I had left the ball, picked it up, and brought it back. For emphasis, I gave my best bring-and-drop right in front of my person's feet. Then I watched as her jaw dropped right down to the ground. Heh, heh! It was a beautiful moment.

You see, with that one simple action, I single-pawedly challenged my person's entire belief system. In that moment, she was questioning how well she really knew me—and wondering how much more I might be hiding from her. Did I really follow the entire conversation? Could it be that I understand everything she says, at all times, and I just choose when to react? Was I offended by her comment and super-motivated to prove myself? Or, was it all just a big coincidence, 'cause I was about to get the ball anyway?

I'm not tellin'!

Was my person annoyed that I might have been ignoring her the whole time? Maybe a little. But the annoyance was dwarfed by her pride in my cleverness. And, remember our discussion about using humor to get out of trouble? This absolutely made her laugh! And remember, if she's laughing, she's not mad.

To this day, my person still tells that story to other peoples. Not only does she find it amusing, but she also enjoys bragging about how smart I am. Granted, she still isn't sure it wasn't just a coincidence. But I know she doesn't think so. Given the choice, peoples will always choose to believe that their dogs are brilliant.

My person also thinks this story illustrates something about my personality: how I am smart but stubborn, sweet but independent, easygoing but strong-willed . . . You get the idea. And she's right. I am a multifaceted canine.

But I digress. To finish out the story: my person had a good laugh, gave me a nice pat on the head, and proceeded to throw the ball. I fetched it three or four times, then ran after it and left it out in the middle of the field again. I returned to my person with a big smile, stretched out in the grass, and completely ignored her elaborate pleas for me to go get the ball. One flash of genius per day is plenty. Always keep them guessing!

Eventually she got the ball herself and we went home and had supper. I caught her looking at me a few times that evening, sizing me up, trying to figure out what was going on in my mind. Unfortunately, the workings of the canine mind are too complex for the average person to comprehend; and my person, though above average in most ways, is no exception. Eventually I took pity on her and gave her a good face licking, which always makes everything better.

I encourage you to try simple games like this to make your peoples question what they know—or think they know—about dog smartness.

Tip 3: Plausible ignorance.

This is a crucial concept: there are boundaries in this world, between acceptable and not-acceptable behavior. It is okay—in fact, I encourage you—to push these boundaries, test them, bend them even, as far as you can. But there is a point at which they will break, and you have officially gone too far.

This is probably one of the most difficult challenges in canine existence. The thing is, you can't know something's off limits until you try it. And there are levels of off-limitedness that you only learn by trial and error. There will be errors. You will cross that line. So when you do, how do you avoid ending up looking at the inside of a wire cage? Two words: plausible ignorance.

The key here is "plausible." If you can make a convincing argument that you did not grasp the wrongness of your action, you may succeed in just bending the line. If, however, you clearly understood how far you were going—and you went there anyway—well, that's another story.

Let's say my person goes out, and she leaves a pile of junk mail on the table. She also leaves a couple of twenty dollar bills. Now, if I were to rip up the money but not the junk mail, my person would be hard pressed to prove motive. Even if I do know that money is more valuable than junk mail, she doesn't know that I know. She will take the blame for leaving the money where I could reach it, leaving me safe in the realm of plausible ignorance.

If, however, she leaves junk mail out on the table and leaves a couple of twenties in a purse, and if I go into that purse and take out the twenties and shred them, leaving the junk mail intact . . . Well, plausibility has pretty much left the building.

You may argue, she still can't prove that I knew the difference between junk mail and cash. She can't prove that I understood the concept of delving into her private possessions, which were being kept safe by a protective purse shell. And she can't prove that the purse didn't fall off the table and spew out the twenties, which just happened to fall right into my mouth.

No, she can't. But she's not an idiot.

Remember, people like to believe that their dogs are smart. So if you stretch plausibility too far, they will not come up with a detailed, crazy story that miraculously lets you off the hook. They will chalk it up to your fabulous brain power. They will be very impressed. And you will get a time out.

You will, someday, go too far. You cannot prevent it any more than you can prevent getting tossed in the bath after you've rolled in poop. What you can control is how your person perceives each misstep that you make. Managing peopleception[7] is a complicated process, but well within the range of canine capability.

What it really comes down to, if you'll pardon the feline-centric expression, is a game of cat and mouse. You know stuff. Your person knows stuff. Some of the stuff your person knows, you also know. But they don't know you know.

_____

7 Author's note: My person informs me that this is not actually a word. I say, it is now! "People's perception" is long and awkward, so I have combined the two into one user-friendly word. I am thinking about calling Webster to have it added to that dictionary thing. After all, he owes me—I shredded my person's copy and she had to buy another one!

In short, a smart dog is like a magician—she never reveals her secrets. Or, in even shorter: they don't know you know they know you know! You know?

Tip 4: Give them a tidbit once in a while.

Peoples like treats as much as dogs do. So it makes sense, since we love our peoples so much, that we should reward them every now and again with something nice. And, since they really enjoy seeing us demonstrate our smarts, this is a great way to do it!

For example, have you ever watched your person trying to find some item that they've misplaced? Probably they're going through every section of the house, getting more and more frustrated that they can't find it. It's not a pretty picture.

Now, if you're like me, you pretty much know where everything is at all times. And if you don't know, you can sniff it out. So picture this: your person is searching for a particular piece of clothing. Unbeknownst to them, but knownst to you, this garment happens to be under the bed.[8] Which is, of course, the one place they are not looking for it.

Somewhere around the third time they've gone through each closet, every drawer, and each laundry pail in the house, they're probably about ready to give up. There's a good chance that they are talking to themselves at this point. This is a clear cry for help. And, as dogs, we must respond!

So, we snap into action, dash into the bedroom, grab the shirt, do a bring-and-drop right in front of our person's feet, and

---

8 Author's note: How it got there is irrelevant.

then watch their face light up! Not only have we helped with their immediate problem, but we have also given them a rare glimpse of our true genius. Clearly, we observed what they were doing, understood the problem, figured out how to solve it, and then did just that. Not too shabby! Your person will rejoice in your intelligence and will proceed to brag about it to everyone they know.

Enjoy the belly rub; you've earned it.

Other opportunities to showcase your smarts will certainly arise; your task is to decide where and when to offer your people a momentary glimpse of greatness.

Doing things before you're asked to do them is quite effective. Has your person ever opened their mouth to say "Sit," only to find you already sitting patiently in front of them? Betcha they thought that was cool!

So what if we take that to the next level? Maybe your person is talking about you with someone, and the other person asks if you know any tricks. Maybe your person is just starting to say, "Well, she knows how to shake paws . . ." and lo and behold, you proffer your paw, ready for shaking, even before the command is officially given. Ditto for rolling over or crawling or whatever other special skills you happen to have listed on your résumé.[9]

This type of thing shows your people that you have good listening skills, that you have good comprehension of what's going on

---

9 Author's note: It is possible to take this too far. One dog I knew was so eager to show off her smarts that every time her person asked for a trick, she frenetically went through every one she knew—rolling over, chasing her tail, standing up, lying down, begging, crawling— and she'd do the whole cycle two or three times. Too much!

around you, and that you are an active participant in the conversation even though you're not speaking. Once you've established this, you are ready to proceed to the next step: join in the conversation.

No, I'm not suggesting that you physically speak people-speak, but there are other ways to have an effective two-way conversation with your peoples. I conversate with mine all the time.

For example, quite often I find myself in the frustrating position of knowing that my ball is under the couch, but being unable to reach under the couch to get it. This is completely unacceptable, whether or not I have any intention of playing with the ball in the immediate future. I need to have complete access to all of my toys, at all times.

Well, it so happens that my person has longer arms than I do, and she is generally willing to get my ball for me. But unless I communicate with her, she doesn't know that's what I'd like her to do. So, I begin a conversation by standing near the stranded ball and whining.

Let me add here that you want to be specific with your whining. Generalized whining accomplishes nothing and, apparently, is annoying to peoples. So I have developed a few distinct whines for use in different situations. For example, I use a plaintive whimper when I need to go outside, an assertive whine when I'd like a biscuit, and an insistent cry[10] when my toy is under the couch. It didn't take too long for my person to catch on and learn which sound represent-

---

10 Author's note: Not to be confused with a *squeal*, which is the sound you make when someone steps on your tail.

ed which situation. She's smart like that.

Sometimes, though, further conversating is necessary. Consider this scenario: I've given my best "I can't get my ball" whine, and my person has responded appropriately by dropping whatever she is doing to come get the ball, but she can't find it. It has rolled deep into a dark corner, where I can smell it but she can't see it. What do we do now?

We communicate! Generally, my person will ask me for better directions. "Where is it? Show me," she might say. And I oblige, by going to the appropriate part of the couch and pointing my nose directly and obviously at the ball's hiding spot. "Oh, it's over there?" she says. She finds my toy, I get to play fetch, and I also get a pat on the head in recognition of my fabulous communication skills.

This simple people-canine conversation demonstrates the foundation for a mutually rewarding system of communication that will serve you well for years to come. Using a combination of sounds and gestures, you can discuss almost anything that's on your mind. The more you do it, the more attuned you and your person will become to each other, and the less effort it will take to share your innermost thoughts and desires. My guess is, once you start, you will be amazed at how much you have to say to each other.

A quick word here about appropriate language. I'm sure you've noticed by now that there are certain words in the people vocabulary that are considered less than polite. If you're like me, you've also realized that while we don't have the ability to produce those exact sounds, we are more than able to approximate the meaning of these words with just the right combination of snarl and bark. A "snark," you might call it.

I believe in speaking my mind. There are moments when a snark is undeniably called for. When I just miss catching my ball in midair and instead it bounces off my head and rolls under the couch, that's a snarking moment. When my person keeps making me roll over again and again and she won't throw the toy until I do it for the thirtieth time, that's a snarker for sure. And at the park, when the Mad Humper *just won't back off*, I'm gonna snark at him.

Just keep in mind that not everything is worth snarking over, and you need to choose your battles. Too much snarking may get you in trouble, and although my person has never followed through with the threat of "washing my mouth out with doggie soap," I would frankly rather not push my luck. So I try to limit my more expressive dialogue to those moments where I feel it's really necessary and to hold my tongue when it isn't. Sometimes a "mooff" is enough.

Snarking is also more effective when it's used prudently. If you snark all the time, people will tune you out. If you use it sparingly, you will get much more bang for your bark. And there is a certain satisfaction in hearing someone asking your person, "Did she just say what I think she said?" And your person responding: "Oh yeah, that's what she said!"

If, like me, you occasionally go a bit too far, you may find yourself in a snarkage situation. Don't worry, this is easily remedied with the "be cute" strategy. Wide eyes and a wagging tongue are your best tools here; use them to ask your person, "How could someone with such an angelic face possibly have said what you thought you heard?" The answer, of course, is that it's simply inconceivable, leaving them no choice but to admit that they must have misunderstood.

Tip 5: Let them think they're in control.

This isn't so much a tip as it is a summary of the entire strategy of this chapter. All of that stuff helps us to keep the balance of control in our favor, while allowing our peoples to think they are pulling all the strings. And that's the way we like it.

In general, we dogs are not physically in control of our lives. With the exception of a few mongo breeds, we are considerably smaller than our peoples, and are therefore at their mercy. They can pick us up anytime they want and move us off of a comfy couch, or into a different room, or onto their own lap. They can hide stuff in high places that we cannot reach. And when we're walking, they are in charge of the leash and, ultimately, of our destination.

With so much power over us, it's no wonder that peoples tend to consider themselves to be in charge. They enjoy the belief that they are the alpha dog. So I say, let them think they are! It makes them happy and hey, what they don't know won't hurt them.

The fact is, alpha dogness has more to do with state of mind than physical prowess. How many times have you seen a vicious Chihuahua growling at a cowering Rottweiler? Does the Rottie think he's small and the Chihuahua is big? No. It's all about the attitude. Similarly, being the bigger critter does not automatically make peoples the alpha dog. They do not control our thoughts, so they are never completely in control.

I am not suggesting all-out rebellion here. In fact, most of the time it suits me just fine to allow my person to take charge. But I am not, nor should you be, a blind follower.

Allowing peoples to take the lead most of the time is a good idea for a couple of reasons: first of all, when you do assert yourself, they won't be expecting it. The element of surprise will give you an edge in getting your way, simply because it will take time for them to catch up with you.

Secondly, peoples are not unreasonable. If you allow them control 90 percent of the time, they may give you more leeway the other 10 percent. They will try to understand the reason for your actions before making a judgment on how to respond. Best scenario is you get permission for what you are doing; worst is, you get to do it for a bit while they think it over.

Ultimately, the decision of how much power to relinquish is yours, and the answer may change from day to day or from hour to hour. But no matter what you decide, the secret to a happy home life is to let the peoples think they are in control. You can rest securely with the knowledge that they are only in control to the extent that you allow them to be.

OPPOSABLE THUMBS
ARE OVERRATED

I'd like to take a moment to address, and challenge, a particularly popular peopleception: that dogs are at a major disadvantage because we do not have opposable thumbs.

Now, I will admit that thumbs are useful things, and certainly there are a few things we dogs simply cannot do. But we are clever creatures, and very creative in using the appendages we do have. I would argue that few tasks are truly impossible for the enterprising canine.

Where there's a will, there's a way.

Let's think about some of the things that might prove challenging for a thumbless creature. Picking things up, for instance. True, I cannot grab hold of a toy with one paw and pick it up; but I can grasp it with my mouth or pull it, two-pawed, to where I want it to be. Score one for the dog.

Now, the idea of being able to pick something up with your

mouth is nothing new. But with this ability comes possibilities, and that's what it's all about: using your innate abilities to redefine the realm of the possible.

One dog I knew, a beautiful white Husky, loved to play ball. But she did not like to catch the ball, nor did she have any interest in fetching it. She wanted to throw the ball. No opposable thumbs? No problem. She picked up the ball in her mouth and gave a good head toss to fling it toward her person, who learned to catch it in midair. Now that's what I call using your head!

Now, what else would you use thumbs for? Perhaps to open packages? That's what teeth are for. Maybe we don't do as neat a job of opening a box, but does that make it any less open? I think not. Pretty much anything my person can get into with her thumbs, I can get into with a good old-fashioned combo of claw and tooth. And I don't need tools; I've got all the cutting instruments that I need right here in my very own mouth.

Ah, yes, you say, but what about doors? You can't open doors, can you? You *must* have opposable thumbs to turn a doorknob. Right?

Well, first let me remind you that not all doors have door-knobs that turn—there are doors with handles that push down, there are doors that slide open, and there are doors with no knobs at all. But yes, those pesky round doorknobs can pose a problem. I have not had a lot of luck with them, using paws or teeth.[1] But this next story proves it is not impossible.

---

1 Author's note: Not for lack of trying.

✶✶✶

The Two Dobies and the Couch—An Inspirational Tale:[2]

Once upon a time, there was a Doberman named Sam. He lived with a people who was a music teacher. The music teacher had a people friend, and one night she came over to visit with her Dobie, Molly. The dogs became fast friends and had a great time playing together while their peoples chatted.

After some time, the peoples decided to go out. Unfortunately, their destination was one of the many locations that discriminate against canine peoples,[3] so they were not able to take the dogs with them. "Hmm," said the man, "perhaps we should devise a plan whereby our dogs will be safe and will not destroy the brand new leather couch while we are gone." The friend agreed, and they came up with an idea.

Now, as you know, the man was a teacher, so it is safe to say that he, himself, was not a stupid man. Nor was the female friend of substandard intellect. But, as is often the case, the dogs were smarter.

The dogs listened carefully while the man crafted his plan. "Why don't we put them in the bedroom," he said, "and close the door. That way, they won't be able to get out, and the living room couch will be safe."

The friend agreed that this was a good idea, and so it came to pass that the dogs were placed in the bedroom together, the bed-

---

2 Author's note: Based on a true story. The names have been changed because I don't know the real ones.
3 Author's note: Theatres, restaurants, and many shops and such for some reason do not allow dogs to cross the threshold. I find this practice highly offensive and speciesist.

room door was closed, and the peoples left the house, secure in the knowledge that the dogs would stay where they were and cause no trouble whatsoever.

But Sam had a different idea. "So here's the plan," he said, once the bedroom door had closed and the peoples had left the building. "We are going to open that door, rip up the couch, and then come back in here and close the door behind us. That will teach them not to leave us alone."

"But how? We have no opposable thumbs," lamented Molly.

"Opposable thumbs, shmapposable thumbs," said Sam. "We don't need no stinking thumbs." They proceeded to use teamwork, teeth, and paws to turn the doorknob, and Sam held the knob while Molly pried open the door. And they were free!

Sam and Molly rejoiced at their freedom, frolicking about the apartment for a while before getting down to the business at hand: teeth tearing cushion, paw pulling foam, until the couch lay in little bits all over the floor. When the destruction was complete, they were both understandably exhausted. They retired to the bedroom for a nap, carefully closing the door behind them until it made that clicking sound that meant it was fully shut. They slept soundly, secure in the knowledge that they had an airtight alibi: they were locked in the bedroom the whole time.

And so it was that the peoples returned to the apartment some hours later and were shocked to find the brand new leather sofa shredded to pieces all over the floor. And even though they knew the dogs did it, they also knew the dogs couldn't have done it!

No opposable thumbs!

Now, I don't know if the peoples really believed the dogs' story: that some other dogs came in and destroyed the house while they, trapped behind that pesky door, were sadly unable to stop the intruders. I would venture to guess that the people saw right through this, recognizing it for the load of crap that it was.

But whether because they were incredibly gullible or because they were incredibly impressed at the sheer genius of their dogs, they did not punish the dogs. They simply sighed, cleaned up the mess, and bought a new—albeit less expensive—couch to replace the destroyed one. Never again did they lock their dogs in the bedroom.

And they lived happily ever after.

***

Ahh, I love that story. I look to it for inspiration, and as a reminder that creativity and determination can get you wherever you want to go. Even if it's through a closed door.

That being said, I want to share one other story with you: a reminder for both canines and peoples that all actions, no matter how well-intentioned, have consequences.

***

The Locked Bathroom Door—A Cautionary Tale:[4]

Once upon a time, my person and I were visiting her father in New York City. I like New York—people everywhere, dogs everywhere, stuff to smell everywhere . . . What's not to like? And I love my grandperson, and all my friends who live in New York, who I only

---

4 Author's note: Also based on a true story.

get to lick a few times a year. So I was happy to be there.

Now, one day, my person had to go out to one of those afore-mentioned speciesist locations, meaning she couldn't bring me along. Which presented a problem, because my grandperson has lots of paper things in his apartment—books especially. And you know I have a particular taste for literature. It tastes very good when I shred it to bits.

Knowing my proclivity for book destruction, and perhaps remembering previous occasions on which I had demonstrated said proclivity while alone in that apartment,[5] my person decided that it would not be a good idea to leave me alone in the same room with all that stuff.[6]

So she made the decision to leave me in the bathroom while she was out. She removed all paper products from the room, provided me with fresh, cool water and a toy, and proceeded to close the door and leave the apartment for what I have been told was about an hour, but seemed to me like a very long time.

Now, it should come as no surprise to you that I was less than ecstatic about this situation. I am a very social creature, and I detest being alone. I wanted nothing more than to join my person on her excursion. And, barring that, I wanted to get out of the bathroom and eat a book. But there I was, behind a closed door, with no opposable thumbs to help me get out.

---

5 Translator's note: Those occasions resulted in the destruction of several issues of the Sunday *New York Times*, an unknown number of books, and one formerly whole (albeit very old) couch.
6 Author's note: Okay, she may have been right . . . but that's beside the point.

So I said to myself, "Self, what should I do?" And I suddenly thought of the story of the two Dobies and the couch. I figured, what the heck? If they could do it, why can't I? And I set out to try and escape from my ignominious incarceration in the bathroom.

Half an hour later, I found myself exhausted and defeated, lying on the bathroom rug, surrounded by splinters from the still-closed door. My best efforts to turn the doorknob with tooth and paw were unfruitful. I suppose I will never know if, with the help of another dog, I could have gotten out; on my own, I could not.

Turns out, though, that my work was not completely without effect. Unbeknownst to me, there was a little device on the door under the doorknob called a "lock," and during my quest for freedom, I turned it—thusly imprisoning myself even more!

This was, I will admit, not my finest moment.

Cut to about an hour later. My person arrived at home and immediately came to open the prison door and let me out. She quickly discovered that the door would not open, and no amount of pushing, banging, or swearing on her part would make it do so. I daresay she was no happier to find this out than I was. In fact, from the sound of her voice through the door, there was some panic happening.

For about the next half hour, she tried everything she could think of to get the door open. This was a noisy process, involving the use of loud machines and a lot of yelling (mainly of my name).

Now, I could hear her yelling my name, and I knew she wanted me to respond; a bark, a whine, or a whimper would have let her know I was all right, trapped but not hurt. I got that concept. But here's the thing: I was tired. I was not in the mood to bark. And, to be completely honest, I did not mind the idea that she was worrying about me. It served her right for shutting me in there in the first place. So, I lay on the cool floor in complete silence and allowed her to think about what she did.

After some time, a nice man came and opened the door,[7] and I came trotting out (well rested by this point) and licked my person's face. I could see that she had, indeed, thought hard about what she did. In fact, she was crying, which made me feel bad, and I licked her face even more. Between the tears and the dog spit, her face was very wet.

And they lived happily ever after.

***

Knowing what I know now, I would have done things differently that day. I still would have shredded the door, but I would have been very careful to stay away from the lock. And, if I were locked in, I'd probably give a little bark to let my person know I was okay. I really didn't mean to scare her quite that much.

Then again, my message got through loud and clear. Never again have I been left alone—in the bathroom or otherwise—in New York City. Mission accomplished.

The thing to remember is that everything we do matters, and even a seemingly harmless act may lead to results we never intended.

---

7 Translator's note: The building's superintendent, who had to come clear across town to let Belle out. To this day, he still laughingly refers to her as "the dog who locked herself in the bathroom."

So, dogs: before you attack that doorknob, think about the fact that you might click the lock of doom! And peoples: before you lock your dog in the bathroom, think about how you'd feel if you couldn't get them back out!

The moral of the story? Cause and effect: it's a bitch.

IF YOU NEVER LEAVE ME,
I WON'T EAT YOUR STUFF

Pretty self-explanatory, right? Yeah, that's what I thought, but years of living with peoples has shown me that this concept is more difficult than it seems. It must be, because no matter how many times I try to train my person on this one, she doesn't get it! I mean, come on: she tells me to sit, I sit. She tells me to stay, I stay. She tells me to roll over, I roll over.[1] I tell her not to leave the house without me . . . and she big fat does it anyway! I don't know how much clearer I can make it.

But, I suppose every creature learns in its own way and at its own pace, and this must be a particularly difficult lesson for her to understand. So, I keep trying—and trying—and trying!—to make it sink in. I will share with you the main methods I use in my training, and I welcome suggestions if any of you have had more luck training

---

1 Author's note: My person tells me it doesn't count if I growl at her while I roll over, but I disagree.

your peoples not to leave you alone. I'm always on the lookout for innovative teaching techniques!

Method 1: Conditioning through negative reinforcement.

Although not necessarily the most effective, this is probably the most widely used method of teaching people not to leave. I will admit that I use this method extensively. Unfortunately, like I said, its effectiveness is questionable at best; but, my guess is that dogs will never stop using this one.

Basically, negative reinforcement means punishment. So, when your person goes out and leaves you behind, you take actions that will be considered unpleasant by your person when they return. For some dogs, this might mean urinating in the house.[2] For others, it might mean chewing up the person's favorite shoes. For me, it means shredding any and all paper within my reach. And maybe plastic. And wood.

Now, in order for negative reinforcement to be effective, you have to differentiate this behavior from normal, everyday doggie behavior (or, if you will, misbehavior). The action you take must be distinctive, directed, and definitive.

If you chew your person's shoes every day just for fun, they're probably not going to catch on that you chewed a particular shoe because they went out without you. It's not a *distinctive* action, and your training efforts will be wasted (although you may have a bit of fun munching the moccasin).

---

2 Author's note: I know I've mentioned this before, but I am revolted by this particular action, and I encourage any of you who do this to stop sacrificing your own cleanliness and dignity.

If you choose a different action each time they leave—shoe chomping one day, paper shredding the next, and bed peeing the third—your people won't understand. They will see these as random acts of misbehavior, not conscious acts directed toward a behavior of theirs that you wish to modify. You must be *directed* in your destruction, so that they can connect your punishment to their crime.

Finally, your action must be *definitive*. This is not the place for half-assed chewing or mediocre shredding. Don't just nibble on the straps—that espadrille must be unwearable. Don't just pull out a page—that book must be unreadable! If you're not willing to go all the way, don't bother, because I guarantee you, it won't work. Nothing is more demoralizing than thinking you've made a bold statement, only to have it go unnoticed or—even worse—laughed at. It's humiliating.

The main downside of using negative reinforcement on peoples is, of course, that you open yourself up to being the recipient of negative reinforcement in return. If you're not prepared to have a time out, you may want to rethink your use of this training method. Just keep in mind that a time out is a small price to pay if your person learns what you are teaching!

Method 2: Conditioning through positive reinforcement.

Positive reinforcement is, as you may have guessed, the opposite of negative reinforcement. So instead of punishing bad behavior, you are rewarding good behavior by taking actions that will please your person.

Your person uses positive reinforcement on you when they

give you a food treat or a toy after you follow a command, or when they pet you and say "good dog." Since peoples use this method so often and so effectively with us, one may surmise that it should work just as well when we use it on peoples.

Of course, the type of reinforcement we give will be different from the type they use with us. We are not likely to offer our peoples a biscuit, or rub their bellies, when they do something nice for us. But that doesn't mean we can't reward them.

Does your person think it's cute when you roll over on your back or rest your paw on their arm? Do they like to have their face licked? Is there a certain sound you make that they just adore? That's a reward! Use your people's favorite behaviors to train them to do your favorite behaviors.

A long while ago I got into the habit of walking over to my person and licking her face right after I get a drink of water. Now, I have no doubt that she would continue to fill my water bowl even if I did not do this. But since she likes to have her face licked, and since I appreciate the effort she puts into keeping my water bowl full and fresh, I think it is a nice way to say "Thank you."

I encourage you to find ways to say thank you to your person. And, once you have discovered how your person likes to be thanked, you can use the same method to train them when they do something you particularly like. When they pet you in just the right spot; when they give you a brand new toy that you simply love; when they play your favorite game with you for hours on end: these are great times to say thanks, and to inspire them to do these things more often.

Unfortunately, positive reinforcement does not seem to be a particularly effective tool in the quest to train my people not to leave me alone. I am very consistent in greeting her exuberantly at the door, standing up on my hind legs, licking her face, and giving her my best full body wag when she comes home. And while I believe she understands what I'm saying, and appreciates my enthusiasm, still she does not stop leaving the apartment without me.

My conclusion is that with this particular training task, you can positive reinforce your ass off, but the reward is associated with "coming home," and doesn't translate to "not leaving in the first place." Apparently people's attention spans are somewhat short; if you don't punish or reward a behavior immediately, they may not make the connection.

Method 3: Putting the shoe on the other paw.

This may be the most effective method I've seen to date, but the problem is that you will have very little control over when, if ever, you get to use it. I just wanted to bring it to your attention so if it does happen, you don't let a golden opportunity go to waste.

The basic concept is pretty simple: How can your person know what it feels like to you when they leave? They can't—unless you show them.

Now, when my person is out for a very long time, there's another person who comes over and takes me out to the park, and feeds me, and loves on me. The term "dog walker" is really inadequate to describe what she does, so let's call her my nanny.

Well, one night a couple of weeks ago, my nanny and I kind

of lost track of time and we got home very, very late. My person had already been home for a couple of hours and she had no idea where we were or when we'd be coming home. She was wandering around the apartment, obsessing about where I was and when I'd be back.

When we did arrive, my person dashed full speed to the door, greeting us with reckless abandon, showering me with kisses and hugs, and repeating over and over again, "You're home, you're home, you're home!"

Sound familiar? Yup, that's pretty much what we do every day when our people leave us alone.

I couldn't have planned it better myself. Literally, as a dog you *can't* plan something like this, because you're not in control of your own comings and goings. But wow, what an amazing training opportunity: to show my person exactly how I feel by allowing her, just for a little while, to feel just as scared and helpless as I do.

Don't get me wrong: I don't want my person to be unhappy or scared, nor would I try to make her feel those things on a regular basis. But this event created a kind of shared experience between us that broadened our mutual understanding and empathy. We had a great conversation afterwards, starting with my person telling me, "I get it now, Belle, I really get it. And I'm sorry." It was a healing moment for both of us.

Does this mean she'll never leave me home alone again? Unfortunately, no. But I understand that she doesn't want me to be unhappy any more than I want her to be unhappy. And she understands just how scary it can be for me not to know when—or if—she's coming home. Hopefully, this new appreciation of each other's perspectives will help us find better coping methods in the future.

Or, maybe I'll just shred some more paper.

Method 4: Desperate times, desperate measures.

So last week my person comes home with a big box. She removes from this box a large metal monstrosity that I hear her describe as a "strong, durable, chew-proof dog gate." Next thing I know, this horrifying object has become a part of the scenery, blocking off two doorways and a portion of the living room wall. Apparently, my person intended this to be a permanent addition to our household decor.

I begged to differ.

As you might imagine, I was offended. Granted, there are two smaller gates that go up every time my person leaves; but at least they come down when she gets back. This one was never going to move, and it had vertical metal bars like a prison—I was being sent directly to the pokey, without a trial. I considered it my moral responsibility to protest such treatment.

But what, you might ask, could I do? After all, if you were paying attention, you know that this was a strong, durable, chew-proof fence. How could I hope to surmount such a barrier as this?

My philosophy is this: "Chew-proof, shmew-proof."

Honestly, there is nothing in this world that is truly chew-proof. At least, if there is, I have not yet found it; therefore, I believe this to be true.

So, using tried-and-true chomping techniques gleaned from

years of practice, I began demolition of the big house. I worked steadily toward my goal each time my person left home, sensing freedom just around the bend, waiting for me to claim it.

It took me four days.

It would be fair to say that my person was not thrilled with this turn of events. I will admit that when she came home and found the gate hanging from its not-so-chew-proof hinges, I scampered down the hall and into our neighbor's apartment for a few minutes. I figured she might need a moment to compose herself before discussing the situation with me. I think this was indeed a good choice on my part.

Once my person collected me from our friends' apartment and cleaned up the remnants of fence, and the paint I scraped off the front door, we sat down and talked. Well, mostly she talked. I had already said everything I needed to say on the subject; my message, it seems, was loud and clear. And while my person may not have agreed with my logic, she couldn't deny that I had a strong argument.[3] And I am pleased to report that, as of the next day, the gate was gone. I do not anticipate that it will return.

So those are the basics on training your people not to leave. Before moving on, however, there is one other point I need to make about the whole separation anxiety thing.[4] I've heard my person saying that since I am so smart, I should have learned by now that she is indeed coming home every day, that I am not going to be aban-

---

3 Author's note: Or at least, strong teeth.
4 Author's note: "Separation anxiety" is the term peoples use to describe "if you never leave me, I won't eat your stuff."

doned, and that while she is out, someone will come and take me out to play even if she cannot do it herself.

You know what? Deep down, I do know that. After all, we have already acknowledged the fact that dogs are highly intelligent creatures. And since I am now a published author, one might argue that I am on the higher end of highly intelligent. So yes, I do know that you always come back, and that my needs are always taken care of. It is my general belief that this will continue to be the case.

You need to understand two things, though. First of all, I am a dog. Dogs live in the present. We remember the past, and anticipate the immediate future; but basically all that matters is the present moment.[5] So even though I know you're coming back later, what I really care about is, are you here *now*?

Secondly, it's not all about me! Don't get me wrong, there are a lot of things in this world that *are* all about me, but this particular one is not.

Part of my species nature as a dog, and my personal nature as a therapy dog, is having great empathy for people's feelings. Whatever a person is feeling—happy or sad, excited or worried, calm or upset—I feel it with them. And if it's *my* person that's feeling it, then I feel it even more.

Now, my person and I have been through a lot together, and I feel it is my job to make sure she is happy, to the very best of my ability. I love my job, and I am very good at it, if I do say so myself.

---

5 Author's note: From what I have observed about the way they worry about all sorts of stuff that hasn't happened yet, it seems to me that peoples could benefit from a more dog-like perspective.

But when she leaves, how can I do my job? If I can't get to her, I can't check on her to see if she's okay. I can't snuggle up to her if she's sad, or distract her with a game of hall ball if she's worried, or anything! And that makes me sad. All I want to do is get to my person, and that's why I scratch at the door and try to dig my way out through the floor. So you see, it's not about me, it's about you!

My person has just pointed out to me that shredding books doesn't really help in my mission of getting to her when she's out. Nor does opening the kitchen cabinets and shredding everything inside them. I tried to argue the point, but let's face it, she's right. So okay, it's a *little* bit about me.

THE DEFINITION
OF CONTENTMENT

There are several ways that dogs express happiness: we smile, we wag our tails—or sometimes, our entire bodies—we make happy sounds, and we pant with joy. Each dog has his or her own preferences, of course; you and you alone know what inspires a full-body wag or makes your leg twitch uncontrollably. But I find that there are a few universal experiences that, for most dogs, will lead to a state of peaceful, blissful contentment. I like to call them contentifiers.

Contentifier 1: I dug my hole, now I'm going to lie in it.

There is a beauty in the digging of holes. From the digging process—determined, focused application of paw and claw—to the smell of the freshly unearthed earth, to the pride of seeing the hole in the ground that you have created all by yourself; it is all very, very good. Then there is the fun of sticking your head in the hole, an activity that is often accompanied by the tantalizing scent of hidden gopher. How cool would it be if you actually caught one![1]

Hole digging is a great game, and one that lends itself to teamwork; some of my best holes in the ground have been collaborative efforts. I know one dog who loves digging so much that she sticks not just her head, but the entire front half of her body in there—she's a brilliant excavator, and an awesome digging partner.

So, once you have dug your hole, and assuming you did not find the elusive gopher, what do you do? Chances are, you're a little bit tired at this point; digging a proper hole takes a good deal of effort. And you're probably a little on the hot side, too. Wouldn't it be great if there were someplace cool and comfy where you could take a little break and revel in your accomplishments?

And therein lies the true beauty of hole digging. When you're done digging, you get to lie in your hole! Depending on your size and your personal positional preferences, you may do this in a number of ways: some dogs curl up in a ball at the bottom of the hole, others stretch out on their back across the hole, and some choose a half-in, half-out approach, with head or leg or butt sticking out like a flag. My preference? The full-belly sprawl, legs straight out in front and back, warm sun on my back, and cool, moist earth on my entire underside. Just thinking about it makes me drool a little.

Next time you're at the park, look at the face of any dog you see ensconced in a freshly dug hole in the ground. That is the face of contentment. Exhausted, satisfied, comfortable contentment.

---

1 Author's note: Okay, I don't actually know what I would do with a gopher if I did catch one, but that's beside the point.

Contentifier 2: The art of seat stealing.

We've all done it: watched and waited until the person, dog, cat, or other creature occupying the perfect perch vacated the premises, and then stolen their seat. Don't try to deny it, you know it's true—dogs are virtuosos when it comes to the art of seat stealing. And it is an art.

Many factors go into determining the most valuable real estate: it's not just about the squishiness of the cushion.[2] The prime place may vary according to your needs at any given time; for example, a lone-standing chair offers excellent napping potential, but a corner of the couch affords more petting possibilities.

Equally important to, if not more important than, a seat's objective comfort level is its popularity among other family members. It's really quite simple: a seat's value rises in direct proportion to how much everyone wants to sit in it.

Therein lies the challenge: how to procure the most comfortable, most coveted seat for your own personal use. And just as importantly—how not to get thrown out of said seat the moment your butt hits the chair.

So how do you get your paws on the prime real estate? First, you must place yourself close enough to the spot that you can get there quickly when the seat is vacated, but not so close that you broadcast your intentions to the seat's occupant. Once you have taken your close-but-not-too-close position, you must stealth watch[3]

---

2 Author's note: Although this is a very important consideration.
3 Stealth watch: intent observation of a subject while not appearing to pay any attention to them.

them. If they see you watching them, they might make more of an effort to protect their turf, and that is exactly what we are trying to avoid.

Now, peoples are overly dependent on their sense of sight, because their senses of hearing and smell are woefully underdeveloped. If a people is watching something closely, they are probably going to stare at it and not look away too much. Since that is the way they experience the world, that is how they expect others to experience it—so they figure, if we are not looking directly at them, we aren't really paying that much attention.

Aha! But we don't have to be looking directly at something to be giving it our full attention. We can hear the slightest shuffling and smell the tiniest bead of sweat. We also process visual images a shade faster than they do, so we perceive movement more quickly and more precisely.[4] We can sense them thinking about moving before they know they're thinking about it. Advantage: dog.

Once you have chosen and staked out your desired spot, it's all about timing. Wait until the person gets up—to go to the bathroom, answer the phone, get a snack, or whatever they need to do—and then pounce onto the seat. Be sure to wait until they are out of the room or fully distracted, and then pounce quickly; otherwise, you run the risk of being caught midpounce, and that's just embarrassing.

If you have done your job properly, your person will return

---

4 Author's note: That's why we are so good at catching uncatchable balls and Frisbees, and why peoples are awed and amazed to see us do it.

to find you curled up or sprawled out, fully ensconced and comfy, exactly where they were sitting just moments before. And this is the key to remaining in the seat—you must look so comfortable, so cute, and so peaceful that they cannot bear to make you vacate the premises. You must fit so perfectly in that seat that anyone would know without a doubt that it was made for you and only you. And you must be so blissfully relaxed that it would seem wrong, even cruel, to disturb you.

If you do this right, here's what you can expect when your person returns and finds you in their seat: they will huff and puff a bit, act indignant, and perhaps scold you a little for your thieving ways. They will stand there for a few moments and wait to see if you voluntarily relocate yourself. They might go so far as to give you a little nudge.[5] They might try and squeeze onto the chair with you. And then they will sigh, get up, and find another seat.

Contentifier 3: Sprawling and "the position."

At the end of the day, nothing beats a good sprawl. Sprawling means different things to different dogs; some dogs sprawl on their backs, some on their bellies, some on their sides; some do all of the above; some invent new and unique sprawling configurations. Though the sprawl may vary, the experience of sprawling is universal, and it remains a great contentifier of dogs everywhere.

Personally, I have a couple of sprawls. One favorite is lying on my belly, with my front and back legs extended fully so my body

---

5 Author's note: If this happens, you aren't looking nearly comfy enough. A properly nestled canine gets no nudge.

is long and flat, every inch of me making contact with the ground beneath me. This can be done anywhere, but it really lends itself to outdoor sprawling. I do this at the park all the time, to feel the full splendor of the cool grass on the soft skin of my belly. I also recommend it indoors on marble floors; it is glorious and really cools you down on a hot day.

Then there is the back sprawl: back on the floor, belly up, legs spread-eagled. Not my favorite position, but it has its advantages, the most obvious of which is that it invites the belly rub. I know a dog who assumes this position and stays that way for ages, figuring that eventually someone will stop and rub her belly. And you know what? Usually someone does! People cannot resist the call of the spread-eagled dog.

I like a good belly rub as much as the next dog, but sometimes I'm not in the mood to flip over onto my back. And truth be told, I find that it is not necessary. I am partial to the semi-back sprawl, where I am really lying more on my side, with my back leg raised so that my belly is exposed. More comfortable, less vulnerable, and easier to spring into action if, say, a tennis ball were to fly out of nowhere begging for me to chase it. And equally effective in tempting the peoples to rub my belly.

The optimum sprawling position is sometimes decided by the location of the sprawl. As I said before, the belly sprawl is excellent for grass and cool surfaces. But I might prefer the back sprawl for the couch, where I could squeeze myself into that space where the back cushions meet the bottom cushions and thus be surrounded by plush goodness.

The couch sprawl, of course, is best when you stretch out and take up as much of the couch as possible. If you're in a good mood, you could leave a corner of the sofa free for your person to sit on. But if not, don't worry; they'll find another chair or sit on the floor.

The bed sprawl is also fun, and again you want to take up maximum space. I recommend the diagonal stretch, head in one corner and body stretched diagonally across the bed to the other corner. This is not only comfortable, it also provides entertainment. It's like seat stealing: as long as you look snug and cozy, I guarantee that your person will not move you from your diago-sprawl. Rather, they will climb in next to you and squish their whole body into one corner of the bed, so as not to disturb you. Always good for a chuckle!

Now you may recall that this section was titled, "Sprawling and 'the position.'" It is my guess that my canine readers know exactly what I mean by "the position," but my human audience might not be quite up to speed, so I will offer an explanation.

Every dog has a favorite position that makes them feel ultra-comfortable, secure, and relaxed; like a little spot of heaven. And while having a position is common to every dog, the specific bodily configuration that becomes "the position" is unique for each of us. There is no rhyme or reason to it, and what is heavenly for one dog may be just okay for another.

"The position" is often incomprehensible to humans because it tends to involve bending in ways that, to them, range from uncomfortable to impossible. Consider my position: I am lying on my back, with my hips relaxed, back legs splayed out, and belly pointing straight up. My front half, however, is twisted to the side so that my front legs are perpendicular to my lower body and the side of my face is on the floor. Sometimes my face is pointing the same way as my front paws; other times, I stretch my neck back so my head forms one straight line with my lower body. And then, when I get bored, I just flip over and rotate my upper body so it's twisted the other way.

I am so relaxed in this position that I can fall asleep that way. My person, however, thinks I'm crazy. She cannot imagine how that could possibly be comfortable and seems to find endless amusement in staring at me in "the position." Which doesn't bother me at all, because I'm far too snug and contented to care.

Dogs, you know what your position is—in fact, I bet your eyes are glazing over a little bit right now just thinking about it. Peoples, if you haven't yet identified your dog's position, just look for those moments when your dog seems idyllic and restful. At these times, ask yourself this: Does that position look remotely comfortable to me? Would I ever do that? Could I even bend that way if I tried? If the answer to these questions is, "Heck, no," then you've probably discovered "the position" for your dog.

A GOOD TIME WAS HAD BY ALL

At the end of the day, you are hopefully tired, full, snuggly, and ready for a good night's sprawl. You have gone to the park and played, worked the crowd, gotten in and out of trouble, licked a bunch of faces, gotten some great belly rubs, and had a nice meal. Peoples, if this is the case, you can trust that your dog is a happy dog. But if you would like some more proof, there are a couple of things you can look for that indicate, without a doubt, that a good time has been had by all.

Indicator 1: Let's talk tongue.

A dog's tongue tells you a lot just by its position and activity. If it's fully inside the mouth, that's a relaxed dog with no particular agenda. If it's sticking out of the front of the mouth, there's probably some licking activity planned—maybe face licking, maybe treat getting, maybe water drinking. If there is panting involved, then we're hot and need to cool down. These are the essential elements of canine tongue language.

On very special occasions, however, you may see a dog with its tongue hanging out the side of its mouth. For a dog, that's like tail wagging to the max. If my tongue is hanging out the side of my mouth, I am giddy with happiness or fatigue. Probably both.

To my dog readers, I say: Imagine the most amazing day at the park or the beach, basking in the sun, wrestling with your friends, playing ball or Frisbee until you can't play anymore, and then licking every face you can reach. Come on, your tongue is hanging out the side of your mouth right now, just thinking about it, right? I know mine is.

Indicator 2: How many pounds of mud did you bring home?

Okay, peoples, before you say a word, remember that we are talking about indicators of dog happiness here, not people happiness. I am fully aware that peoples are not so much crazy about lugging home half of the park. But dogs are!

Collecting pounds of mud in our fur is enjoyable for so many reasons: the feel of it, the smell of it, and the sheer pride of it. It's like a status symbol. When you see a really mud-covered dog at the park, take a look at the other dogs in the vicinity. You'll see it in their eyes: the longing for mud of their own, the admiration for a job well done, and the hope that someday soon, they will be so gloriously filthy. Check out the muddy rascal again. Note the spring in his step, the pride in his prance. The muddier, the merrier.

The only problem with bringing home several pounds of mud is the inevitable bath. I have resigned myself to the fact that my people and I are never going to see eye to eye on this issue. I will continue to get slimed, because it is what I have to do. They will continue to throw me in the tub and wash off my hard-earned earthen coating, because it's what they have to do. It's okay because I know that, bath or no bath, I achieved great sludginess. And because, let's face it, we both know I'm gonna do it again!

Indicator 3: Please step over the dog.

I remember when I was a puppy—I mean, like six weeks old or so—and I could sleep through anything. I'd play and play and play and then . . . I'd pass out. And out meant out. People could talk, walk, tap dance, or play the bongos right next to me, and as long as they didn't step on me, I would not wake up until I was good and ready to wake up.

Then after a couple of months, I started to be more aware of my surroundings, even in my sleep. If my person moved, I would hear it, and I'd get up and follow her. If she opened a bag of dog treats, I'd smell them and run over to get one. If she turned on the lights, I'd sense that too and—bing!—I was awake.

As I've matured, I've become more selective in what I will or will not sleep through. I can still hear, smell, and feel things that are going on around me; but I also know what requires immediate action and what can wait. So depending on what's going on, and on how tired I am, I may or may not abandon a good snooze.

After a really great day, though, all bets are off. A blissful and wacky-active day of play is like an instant fountain of youth, returning the average adult dog to puppyhood for a couple of hours. These are the times when we fall asleep on the floor, completely oblivious to everything around us, and simply trust that you will please step over the dog.

***

Okay, so it's the end of the day. You have been mud-covered and bathed, you are unconscious on the floor, and your tongue is hanging out of your mouth as you relive the day in your dreams. Your person is cooking dinner, but you are too tired to care . . . although it smells good . . . really good . . . hmm . . . Okay, maybe we could wake up now, you think. You open one eye. Then the other. Then you stretch out your front legs, and your back legs, and give your whole body a good head-to-butt shake. And now . . . Well, now what?

Supper, cuddling, and do it all again tomorrow!

And a good time was had by all.

ABOUT THE AUTHOR

Belle is a mixed-breed dog who came from the humblest of beginnings: at the tender age of six weeks, she was living on the streets of south Los Angeles. The people who were taking care of her (using the term loosely) did not want her and gave her to a Los Angeles police officer who happened to be walking by. Luckily, they picked the right officer, because he and his wife are avid dog lovers and often rescue strays in the course of their travels. Through these caring people, Belle found her forever home.

While Belle's exact heritage remains a mystery, best guesses are that she is part Labrador Retriever, part Border Collie, and part . . . other stuff. Her determination to lick faces and her long, darting tongue have led some to suggest that she is part snake; they have also earned her the nickname Mrs. Kisses.

Belle has the intelligence and ingenuity of Snoopy, the sweetness of cotton candy, and the destructive capability (when left alone with the Sunday paper) of the Tasmanian Devil. Ninety-nine percent love and one percent attitude, she knows what she likes and she believes in speaking her mind.

Belle's outgoing nature and enthusiasm for meeting new people made her a perfect candidate to become a therapy dog. The rescued became the rescuer, and Belle has loved and licked many children and seniors around the Los Angeles area.

You can keep up with Belle's latest musings at:

www.dogonlyknows.com

And be sure to follow her on Facebook and Twitter:

www.fb.com/dogonlyknows, and **www.twitter.com/thedogonlyknows**

ABOUT THE TRANSLATOR

Terry Kaye is a professional writer, actress, and singer whose career has taken her across the United States, Canada, and Europe. Look for her wiping up ghostly ooze in the upcoming thriller *We Go On*, starring Annette O'Toole. She also starred as Claire in the pilot episode of *Forbidden Doors—The Web Series*, based on the popular series of novels by Bill Myers.

Currently a Los Angeles resident, Terry is a New York City native and maintains that East Coast edge. She describes herself as a New Yorker who happens to spend a lot of time out of town.

Terry is a lifelong dog lover and has always known that she "speaks dog," but never had her own canine companion until her fiancé showed up on her doorstep with Belle, a little black fluff ball with a white goatee. It was love at first sight, and the rest, as they say, is history.

ABOUT THE ILLUSTRATOR

Kat McDonough makes lots of art, all of the time. Her favorite subjects are furry creatures and children. Born and raised a Jersey girl, she now lives in Los Angeles with her husband and son. She's a graduate of Otis College of Art and Design in Los Angeles. Her work has graced the walls of galleries, private collectors' homes, and various publications.

You can see more of her art at:

www.katmcdart.com

CPSIA information can be obtained
at www.ICGtesting.com
Printed in the USA
LVOW01s0455300916
506778LV00002B/8/P